Digital Intelligence

A framework to digital transformation
capabilities

Dr Mehmet Yildiz

Distinguished Enterprise Architect

First Edition, September 2019
Copyright © Dr Mehmet Yildiz
Publisher: S.T.E.P.S. Publishing Australia
P.O Box 2097, Roxburgh Park, Victoria, 3064 Australia
info@stepsconsulting.com.au
Edited by Mark Longfield

Disclaimer

Table of Contents

Chapter 1: Introduction

Purpose of this book

I authored this book because dealing with intelligence, and the digital world is a passion for me and wanted to share my passion with you. In this book, I aim to provide compelling ideas and unique ways to increase, enhance, and deepen your digital intelligence and awareness and apply them to your organisation's digital journey particularly for modernisation and transformation initiatives. I used the architectural thinking approach as the primary framework to convey my message.

Based on my architectural thought leadership on various digital transformation and modernisation engagements, with the accumulated wealth of knowledge and skills, I want to share these learnings in a concise book hoping to add value by contributing to the broader digital community and the progressing initiatives.

Rest assured, this is not a theory or an academic book. It is purely practical and based on lessons learned from real enterprise transformation and modernisation initiatives taken in large corporate environments.

I made every effort to make this book concise, uncluttered, and easy-to-read by removing technical jargons for a broader audience who want to enhance digital intelligence and awareness.

Upfront, this book is not about a tool, application, a single product, specific technology, or service, and certainly not to endorse any of these items. However, this book focuses on architectural thinking and methodical approach to improve digital intelligence and awareness. It is not like typical digital transformation books available on the market. In this book, I do not cover and repeat the same content of those books describing digital transformations. My purpose is different.

What distinguishes this book from other books is that I provide an innovative thinking framework and a methodical approach to increase your digital quotient based on experience, aiming not to sell or endorse any products or services even though I mention some prominent technologies which enable digital transformation, for your digital awareness, intelligence, and capabilities.

Audience

When I was authoring this book, my conversations were towards digital leaders who may have taken the plunge for the enormous responsibility of digitally transforming large enterprise organisations. I pictured a typical digital leader trying to make sense of the transforming environment. Therefore, this book can be an ideal source for digital leaders who want to increase their understanding of these complex environments and increase their digital intelligence learning from the experience of someone who diligently observed and engaged in these environments. The guidance in this book can jump-start the thinking process for digital capabilities.

The target audience for this book is primarily Digital Leaders, IT Architects, Specialists, Program Managers, Transformation Executives including CTO- Chief Technology Officer, CDO - Chief Digital Officer, CIO -Chief Information Officer, and Head of Enterprise Technologies - who engaged in and are responsible for substantial enterprise modernisation and digital transformation programs.

As an educative resource, this book can also be useful for students studying in disciplines related to digital technologies.

My Journey to Digital Intelligence

I am passionate about intelligence. More than anything else, as a personal interest, intelligence is a thrilling and uplifting subject for me. Strangely enough, I am attracted to intelligent people, animals, and machines. It became such an obsession that I couldn't hold it anymore to myself and wanted to share my thoughts and passion with my readers, hoping that this madness can add some value to them.

My cravings to understand human and machine intelligence started in earlier years of my tertiary studies in informatics and intensified with my doctoral studies in cognitive science which covered both natural and artificial intelligence. I am still obsessed with this topic hence couldn't help myself to share my thoughts with a broader audience.

Extending human intelligence using technology intelligence has been a particular interest over the years. Therefore, I continued my studies and research in the area and chose a profession to deal with both human and machine intelligence in a broader sense and an integrated context.

My brain loves structures and patterns since I have been a technologist and practising as an Enterprise Architect dealing with people, technology, process, tools and integration of heterogeneous systems. These engagements required a considerable amount of intelligence to achieve successful outcomes in commercial settings.

Like the universe itself, then out of nowhere, digital intelligence came into the picture to extend my intelligence to a different perspective. Since then, I keep swimming in the digital ocean daily and find it quite refreshing even though it may be risky and harmful for my health at times; but I love it. Now you may ask it rightly, where is the intelligence in this paradox.

This extended perspective to the digital arena with passion helped me to deal with complex and rapid change. I became a more flexible and nimbler person. Dealing with digital matters expanded my horizons and enabled me to engage in fascinating intellectual activities in global settings.

Large organisations that I work for are substantially challenged with rapid change in technology and increasing demands of consumers in this digital era. Every large organisation that I worked for had some digital transformation and modernisation programs to some extent at the enterprise level. These organisations needed passionate leaders to transform them. I was in the right places in the right times.

Digital technologies in enterprises have multiple dimensions spanning to many domains. These domains are tightly interrelated; hence, a minor change in one domain can reflect in many others. Dealing with these interrelated domains and their components require substantial digital intelligence.

In this book, I aim to explain these challenges in the most straightforward format methodically and provide insights based on practical architectural thinking approach to deal with them. Some of the points may sound trivial or boring, but each point I raised can have critical implications and make a significant impact on the success or failure of the digital endeavours. Let's set the scene with the fundamentals of intelligence and start our conversation!

Chapter 2: Fundamentals of Intelligence

Purpose

Before starting to discuss digital intelligence, we need to understand and reach consensus on the meaning and fundamentals of intelligence to bring us all on the same page. With a shared understanding of intelligence, my points and observations can make betters sense to you to enjoy and benefit the content in this book.

Meaning of Intelligence

I am sure you know what intelligence means as you purchased this book and started reading it. However, my architectural mind does not allow me to explain a topic without defining it to my audience. It is a strange habit. With all due respect, I attempt to define the intelligence so that the subsequent chapters can make a better sense to you.

The standard definition of intelligence is the ability to acquire knowledge and skills and apply them as needed. This simple definition can be unfolded using various associated terms and concepts crossing and overlapping multiple disciplines creating different meanings for intelligence.

Cognitive science is one of the leading disciplines dealing with human intelligence. Knowledge and information management are the other disciplines, also covering human intelligence to some extent. Intelligence also relates to disciplines dealing with human brain and mind. Psychology, Psychiatry and Neuroscience are some of the most prominent examples.

Standard foundational terms related to intelligence are intellect, reasoning, judgement, mental capacity, brainpower, smartness, astuteness, brilliance, discernment, insights, perceptiveness, and comprehension. These terms all relate to intelligence in some ways. I used some of these terms to explains some points related to digital intelligence.

The above terms mainly revolve around human IQ (intelligent quotient). However, intelligence goes beyond IQ and covers the emotional, social, and spiritual aspects of human beings. Therefore, we come across the emerging disciplines such as emotional intelligence, social intelligence, and spiritual intelligence. All these intelligence types interrelate for our interactions in society. Let's take the term intuition as an example; it can relate to cognitive, emotional, social and spiritual aspects.

In our day to day life, we can describe intelligence using terms and phrases such as sharpness, quickness of mind, astuteness, giftedness, alertness aptness, wit, cleverness, canniness, smartness, talent, and even braininess in informal settings.

Most of the times, the above adjectives are used to describe people's IQ rather than their other intelligence aspects. I witnessed in some situations; for example, some people described a talented employee as the woman or man of superintelligence even though talent can be related to social and emotional capabilities of a person too.

After this brief introduction to the meaning of intelligence to bring us on the same page, now let's touch on digital intelligence, which is the primary theme of this book, assuming it is your main reason to purchase this book.

What is Digital Intelligence

Quite frankly, I have not come across a standard definition for digital intelligence so far. Even more depressingly, I have not seen an established body of knowledge or substantial publications directly researching the phenomena of digital intelligence.

However, does it mean that digital intelligence doesn't exist? Not in my humble opinion. Interestingly, during my literature search, I reviewed a few case studies using the term "Digital Intelligence" and skimmed some marketing brochures, articles, and blogs discussing digital quotient, which sound promising. I thought at least better than nothing!

I take the plunge and make an effort here to define digital intelligence as a new term at the most fundamental level to provide an understanding of this term for clarity so that we set the context for the book. Just to level set, my aim here is to create awareness and show some thought leadership, not to credit myself unrealistically as an expert in the field as the field does not fully exist yet or it is just about to emerge.

My definition of digital intelligence, at a high level, is the ability to convert or represent the physical world in digital format. Even though it sounds straightforward, these two critical verbs (convert and represent) have a loaded meaning and create enormous complexity. The terms - convert and represent- can extend to multiple disciplines and domains. Ability covers a broad spectrum of process, people, tools, and technologies.

Physical and digital are two different worlds with dissimilar entities. They have their inherent capabilities and limitations. By using computer science and engineering, we found ways to represent the physical world in digital formats. Therefore, they are related and can enhance each other's scope.

When we are exploring general intelligence in the previous section, we mention that intelligence is the ability to acquire knowledge and skills and apply them as needed. We can transfer this definition to defining digital intelligence. In this case, we may claim that digital intelligence is the ability to acquire and apply digital knowledge and skills encompassing the digital world. The digital world consists of various processes, technologies, tools, techniques, methods, and approaches.

There are one-way, two-way, or multiple-way relationships amongst these components. Our digital intelligence, in this case, also relates to an understanding of all relationships for these components and their sub-components. This understanding involves an enormously complex task hence require in-depth knowledge of the digital world and cross-discipline skills to make sense of this fascinating world.

In other words, to be digitally intelligent, we need to have in-depth knowledge of the process and acquire practical skills relevant to the digital disciplines. In the next chapter, we discuss how architectural thinking can help us gain awareness and increase our digital intelligence.

Chapter Summary and Take Away Points

The standard definition of intelligence is the ability to acquire knowledge and skills and apply them as needed.

Digital intelligence, at a high level, is the ability to convert or represent the physical world in digital format.

Physical and digital are two different worlds with dissimilar entities. They have their inherent capabilities and limitations.

To be digitally intelligent, we need to have in-depth knowledge of the digital process and acquire practical skills relevant to the digital disciplines.

Chapter 3: Architectural Thinking Framework to Unfold Digital Intelligence

Purpose

The purpose of this chapter is to provide an overview of architectural thinking approach and how it relates to digital intelligence. From my experience, architectural thinking can be used as a robust framework to gain digital knowledge, unfold the mystery of digital intelligence, and increase our digital intelligence by providing a structured approach.

This structured and methodical approach can serve as a checklist to measure our digital intelligence. Our brains love structure and patterns. Using architectural thinking principles as a checklist ensures that we cover essential factors and steps in the thinking process for the digital world. This structured thinking process can be invaluable in our digital pursuits.

Vision

In architectural thinking, life starts with a vision. In other words, as a top-down approach, architectural thinking mandates setting the vision first. Vision is being able to think about the future with creative imagination and human wisdom.

Vision sets the scene and shows us where we want to be in the future. Even though everyone has a vision, a productive and strategic vision is a leadership capability and requires a substantial amount of intelligence, knowledge, skills, and experience. As a digital leader, I assume you have a compelling vision for your organisation's transformational journey.

Practising vision in digital engagements can help us think strategically. Visionary thinking can be used to improve our intelligence as it involves multiple mental attributes and processes. Now that we covered vision briefly let's move the next important point, strategy.

Strategy

Once we have a compelling vision for the digital world, it is time to set the strategy. We need to know where we are now on the digital journey and where we want to go. Our digital strategy helps us reach our destination using a master plan. The master plan can be a high-level roadmap to take us to the destination we set. You may call it a map too.

Similar to visionary thinking, strategic thinking also can help us increase our digital intelligence as far as our strategies related to digital matters such as the adoption of digital progress leading to transformation. Our digital strategy can have many requirements.

Requirements

Any digital endeavour has its requirements. Indeed, many requirements! Requirements can have multiple facets, and they are not straight forward. Therefore, understanding requirements from all angles are critical. Requirements involve multiple processes and stakeholders.

Both users and systems have their requirements. There are different requirements for different kinds of users — for example, internal and external users, technical, executive, and management users. Systems also have their unique requirements. We can call them technical, support, and operational requirements. In general, requirements can be functional and non-functional.

Requirements gathering for digital endeavours are an end to end process such as collecting, analysing, clarifying, tracking, validating, and using. These are intellectual activities requiring digital intelligence. Talking of intelligence, using the acronym SMART to characterise requirements have been instrumental. SMART stands for specific, measurable, actionable, realistic and traceable. These five attributes can help increase the quality of requirements. To better understand requirements, especially from the user perspective, we need to deal with use cases.

Use Cases

Related to requirements, understanding the use cases for digital solutions are essential architectural thinking skills. Dealing with use cases require different thinking modes, such as looking at things from the user's perspective. Observing and being an observer at the same time is a critical mental capability.

More specifically, a use case is a specific situation depicting the use of a product or service of a solution by the consumers. We develop use cases from the users' perspective. We need to understand how the consumers are intended to be using a particular component or aspect of the solution.

Usually, the functional requirements can help us to formulate the use cases. Alternatively, in some circumstances, use cases help formulate the functional requirements. Use cases and requirements are interrelated. We need to analyse them together; not in isolation.

Some selected users can help us understand the use cases when we interact with them. We need to ask questions to the users and obtain their feedback on how they are intended to use a function that is expected to be in the solution document.

In general, overall solution use cases need to be defined and elaborated with the input from all stakeholders of the solution; not just end-users.

There may be different use cases for different stakeholders.

Use cases can also be determined based on roles and personas in a solution. Personas represent fictitious characters based on our knowledge of the users in the solution. Identifying personas and use of them in our use case development and requirements analysis can be beneficial.

Current and Future State

After understanding the requirements and use cases, we need to apply them to the current state. The current state shows us where we are now. By understanding the current state, we set future state and develop a roadmap to reach the target goals. This architectural thinking approach applies to any digital solution that we engage in daily. This structured approach is instrumental in digital transformation initiatives.

Feasibility

Architectural thinking can guide us to think the feasibility of our digital solution roadmap looking at the risks, dependencies and the constraints on the way. This assessment process covering all aspects of our solution requires substantial thinking capability. Developing a comprehensive viability assessment can help us mitigate critical risks, resolve existing issues, address challenging dependencies. Missing this critical step in our thinking can result in dire consequences in the long run.

Trade-offs

Most of the time, assessing viability also require making a considerable number of trade-offs to reach optimal solution outcomes. When making trade-offs, we need to consider critical factors, such as cost, quality, functionality, usability and many other non-functional items.

We make trade-offs to create a balance between two required yet incompatible items. In other words, a trade-off is a compromise between two options. It is possible to make a trade-off between quality and cost for particular items. We make some of the architectural trade-offs to deal with uncertainties. For these types of trade-offs, techniques such as combining, comparing, and contrasting can be beneficial.

Decisions

Each trade-off also requires architectural decisions. These crucial decisions can have substantial implications for the success or failure of the digital solution. We need to make architectural decisions very carefully as each decision can have a severe impact and multiple implications. Some implications can be cost-related, while others can relate to performance, availability, security and scalability. We need to communicate architectural decisions with multiple stakeholders.

Context

After making the decisions, another challenging task is to provide a representative picture of the solution in a single page. It is usually called the solution context showing the critical dependencies. This abstract thinking ability is an example of intelligence that we add to the digital solution process. Setting the context for any solution help us communicate it to relevant stakeholders in an efficient manner. Context adds clarity to understanding the solution.

Models

Models are significant work products in architectural solutions. A model is the proposed structure typically on a smaller scale than its original. Once we draft the solution at an abstract level and our stakeholders understand it, the next important step in the architectural thinking process is to represent the abstract level in further details by describing each component and the relationships.

Describing abstract representations in concrete details also requires a great deal of mental exercise, including dealing with multiple patterns, which can stimulate our thinking abilities.

This chapter concludes the high-level architectural thinking approach that we can use to increase our digital intelligence. Now, let's delve into digital complexity which is another important topic related to digital intelligence.

Chapter Summary and Take Away Points

Architectural thinking can be used as a robust framework to gain digital knowledge, unfold the mystery of digital intelligence, and increase our digital intelligence by providing a structured approach.

Vision sets the scene and shows us where we want to be in the future. Even though everyone has a vision, a productive and strategic vision is a leadership capability and requires a substantial amount of intelligence, knowledge, skills, and experience.

Our digital strategy helps us reach our destination using a master plan. The master plan can be a high-level roadmap to take us to the destination we set.

Both users and systems have their requirements. There are different requirements for different kinds of users.

Requirements gathering for digital endeavours are an end to end process such as collecting, analysing, clarifying, tracking, validating, and using.

Dealing with use cases require different thinking modes, such as looking at things from the user's perspective. Observing and being an observer at the same time is a critical mental capability.

By understanding the current state, we set future state and develop a roadmap to reach the target goals.

Architectural thinking can guide us to think the feasibility of our digital solution roadmap looking at the risks, dependencies and the constraints on the way.

A trade-off is a compromise between two options. When making trade-offs, we need to consider critical factors, such as cost, quality, functionality, usability and many other non-functional items.

We need to make architectural decisions very carefully as each decision can have a severe impact and multiple implications. Some implications can be cost-related, while others can relate to performance, availability, security and scalability.

Setting the context for any solution help us communicate it to relevant stakeholders in an efficient manner. Context adds clarity to understanding the solution.

A model is the proposed structure typically on a smaller scale than its original. Describing abstract representations in concrete details also requires a great deal of mental exercise, including dealing with multiple patterns, which can stimulate our thinking abilities.

Chapter 4: Digital Complexity

Purpose

Dealing with complexity requires extensive intelligence. Considering the context of digital intelligence, the purpose of this chapter is to point out the complexity as one of the most significant challenges related to digital engagements. Once we understand the complexity, the next step is to find effective ways to deal with complexity. As you may guess, I'd propose a structured approach to deal with complexity.

Enterprise Environments

We know that enterprise environments can be extremely complex with multiple layers of systems, technologies, tools, and processes. However, these are just tips of the icebergs. The more significant part of the iceberg, the real challenge, is dealing with people in the enterprise, especially multiple stakeholders with different roles, responsibilities, and confusing agendas. Coupling systems and people can add extra complexity to the enterprise environments. You got the picture!

Managing Complexity

There are different approaches and techniques to manage complexity in enterprises transforming to digital goals. In this section, I provide a quick and generic approach to deal with complexity.

The most common technique is simplifying complexity by using a partitioning approach. This technique applies to both systems and people. To simplify complexity, we can divide, subdivide, segregate, or apportion the systems, objects, or components, or teams to smaller units.

The process of partitioning refers to making smaller parts of an astronomical object like a transforming enterprise. Let's say that we are dealing with an extensive network system in the organisation. Dealing with such an extensive system can be daunting. In this case, we partition the overall network to smaller parts such as a wide-area network or a local-area network. Then we can further partition the wide-area network from tools perspectives such as routers, switches and other devices. Then, dealing with the segmented system can be more efficient and faster.

Once we partition an overarching system, then we can start simplifying it by looking at the quantity. One way of simplifying a system is reducing the number of repetitive constituents. Take the number of servers, for example, looking at a thousand units of servers, and ten servers can make a massive difference.

Another technique could be moving an item from a large group of the clustered items but still, keep the relationship to preserve its core identity. I offer a chapter later on the importance of simplification for enterprise modernisation and digital transformations as simplification is a critical success factor.

After partitioning and simplifying, the following useful method is iterating. Probably you heard a lot about this term while working with agile methods. Iteration is progressing activities in smaller steps and chunks. Iteration is one of the best approaches to deal with complexity and uncertainty.

Moving with iterative steps, we can achieve some small results. If the small result is positive, we make progress and go to the next iteration. If the result is negative, we fail but learn how not to do it and try another iteration.

The positive side of this negative result is that we fail cheap, and we fail quickly. Failing cheap and quickly don't make a big difference from a financial and project schedule perspective. Paradoxically, failing cheap and quick provide financial gains.

We can remember these three basic methods using daily examples such as we have separate teams for different functions at work; this is partitioning of teams. We only belong to a single nation; this is a simplification. We plan for a school or certification exam chapter by chapter; this is iteration. There are also different tools that we use for these techniques. We cover them in subsequent chapters of this book.

Chapter Summary and Take Away Points

Dealing with complexity requires extensive intelligence.

The most common technique is simplifying complexity by using a partitioning approach. We can divide, subdivide, segregate, or apportion the systems, objects, or components, or teams to smaller units.

One way of simplifying a system is reducing the number of repetitive constituents.

Another technique could be moving an item from a large group of the clustered items but still, keep the relationship to preserve its core identity.

After partitioning and simplifying, the following useful method is iterating.

Chapter 5: Financial Intelligence for Digital

Purpose

Arguably, the financial aspect of digital transformations can be the most important one. Even if we create a paragon of architecture with flawless designs, if the solution is economically not viable and it does not produce a compelling return on investment, it cannot be considered as successful. Therefore, financial intelligence for digital transformation is mandatory and should be a priority objective. The purpose of this chapter is to provide a high-level view of digital cost and value propositions. Understanding the financial aspects makes valuable contributions to our digital intelligence.

Digital Cost Awareness

Everything in enterprise transformation generates substantial cost. There are known and hidden costs. It is relatively more comfortable to deal with the known costs; we can apply some logic and resources to address them. However, the real challenge is to deal with the hidden costs.

Hidden costs are the more significant part of the proverbial iceberg. Even though financial teams manage the cost, the technical team need to find ways to make digital solutions inexpensive, affordable and lowering the cost gradually without compromising quality. Quality considerations are the critical requirements of digital transformation initiatives.

Quality and Cost Concerns

There is a common perception that making solutions cost-effective without compromising quality is not possible. The reason is that we must make a considerable number of trade-offs in the architecture and technical development phases. I partially agree with this statement. There are many challenges and factors to be considered to achieve this goal. Our approach makes a difference.

As digital leaders, we can contribute to reducing the solution costs by making trade-offs with a methodical and collaborative approach. For example, we can obtain collaborative input by bridging business and technology stakeholders. We can apply an agile approach and other innovative ways such as automation and standardisation to repetitive and resource-hungry components.

We can increase the quality of the solutions by applying professional diligence, architectural rigour, delivery agility, smart collaboration across multiple teams, and harvesting re-usable materials. These principle-based and cost reduction approaches are critical to maintain and increase quality. Increasing quality can have a favourable effect on the financial viability of the solutions.

Bill of Materials

Simple yet a powerful impact on cost control is related to Bill of Materials in digital transformation programs. Bill of Materials refers to hardware, software and services costs. As digital leaders, we can participate in cost model development proactively. For example, we can help develop a solution Bill of Materials once we set the solution strategy and complete all high-level design artefacts.

Beware that there may be tremendous pressure from project managers and procurement staff to generate an upfront Bill of Materials due to demands of the project lifecycle. However, we can point out that without an approved architecture and design, we cannot commence purchasing materials.

This assertive and straightforward intelligence from technical team members can save a considerable amount of funds to the enterprise modernisation and transformation programs or save wasting well controlled and tight budgets in this economic climate. Unfortunately, I witnessed on several occasions, millions of dollars of materials purchased upfront and wasted due to changes in architecture and designs. This lesson learnt worth consideration.

Infrastructure and Maintenance Costs

There can be extensive infrastructure and maintenance costs associated with large data centres, server farms, mobile devices, storage units, data processing tools, analytics machines, and hosting in multi-Clouds.

These foundational infrastructure components are essential to make digital enterprise solutions viable. However, a single failure or defect in a device or a group of devices serving the consumers via these high-end technologies can adversely affect the service levels hence could lead to high costs for the service providers.

Availability and Performance Costs

Availability and performance of the systems are the significant factors to address punitive service levels. One way of intelligence to address these risks is the introduction of automation to service management.

Automated SLAs can detect low availability and poor performance. These automated SLAs trigger the rules and force the organisations breaching the agreements pay the contractually agreed penalties.

The downtime is the most critical factor for generating excessive penalties. The longer the systems are down, the higher the penalties. Our contribution to availability and performance by taking necessary measures can make a substantial difference in cost management. We discuss the implications of SLAs in the next section.

Service Level Agreements

Service downtime costs can be very high based on agreed rates and cause excessive penalties when accumulated for service-level breaches by organisations. Service Level breaches also have a strategic adverse effect on an organisation's product and services. For example, downtimes in services or defects in products can result in poor client satisfaction. If we also look at from the consumer perspectives, they lose business due to service downtimes. It is a lose-lose scenario even though the consumer organisations are compensated with SLA penalties paid by the service providers.

We need to pay attention to the SLAs from the nascent stages of the digital solution life cycle. The higher the quality of the solutions, the easier it is for SLAs to meet when the solutions are in production and the operational state. The rigour for quality in each phase can positively contribute to deal with SLA risks.

Some of the key considerations to address SLA issues could be autonomous condition monitoring and remote maintenance. There are specialist solutions regarding these trending techniques. It can be useful to assign automation and standardisation specialists for the design of these unique features in our digital solutions.

Service level management is also crucial in digital initiatives. To put this into a practical perspective, one of the biggest fears of the business executives is the impact of poor performance and availability problems damaging their organisations' client satisfaction and compromising business revenues.

To address the risks associated with this valid business concern, digital leaders need to pay special attention to SLA strategy, planning, design and implementation in an integrated way. A proactive and effective SLA management is one of the key areas where digital intelligence makes a real difference in cost management.

Digital Systems

Digital transformations are long journeys moving the enterprises from chaos to coherence. The transformation process includes every aspect of the enterprise. For the scope of this book, we focus on digital systems. Even though digital systems look only a tiny bit of an organisation in overarching enterprise, this domain by itself can be gigantic, especially for the large organisations.

Enterprise digital systems can include business IT processes, business data, business applications, IT infrastructure, and IT service delivery. These domains can even be more complicated with the addition of geographical factors such as adding multiple countries to the equation.

One of the essential workaround solutions for dealing with this complexity is to modernise these primary domains iteratively in parallel. Let's review the methodical approach that I present in the next section.

Methodical Approach to Cost Management

The digital solution leaders need to follow a methodical approach to manage the cost and contribute to the solution viability and profitability. Both a top-down and bottom-up approach must be applied depending on the needs.

At the top tier, we see the business and IT processes, and at the bottom tier, we see IT infrastructure. These two domains can independently be transformed using parallel activities. However, an integrated approach is essential as there can always be dependencies from multiple angles in both top-down and bottom-up approaches.

Once an organisation has an approved transformation strategy, then the digital leaders refine the strategy and convert it to clear architectural and technical formats. The strategy document is a critical artefact to bring all parties and stakeholders on the same page. Then the digital solution leaders identify the critical dependencies among these domains based on the short term, midterm and long-term considerations.

By using the strategy and considering the dependencies, the digital solution leaders need to develop a high-level roadmap to inform the sponsoring executives. This roadmap can indicate the key outcomes, timelines and a ballpark cost for the overall modernisation and transformation activities. These indications initially can be at a very high level as there may be many factors affecting timelines, resources, and associated cost.

Once the roadmap for the digital transformation is set the solution leaders need to make a comprehensive viability assessment considering the current state of the scoped initiatives, their indicative future state and the strategies to reach the end state. This viability assessment must include key risks, constraints, and dependencies. The viability assessment can be the most informative tool a digital solution lead can provide to the sponsoring executives to make informed decisions.

After review and approval of the viability assessment, the digital solution leaders delve into collecting the high-level requirements of the solutions based on the domains we mentioned earlier. As dealing with the requirements of those domains can be daunting, the digital solution leaders can delegate the requirements collection process with the domain and program architects, technical specialists, and business analysts based on their skills set relevant to the types of requirements.

In this phase, the role of the digital solution lead is to coordinate and facilitate the requirements management team, which can consist of multiple architects, technical specialists, and business analysts.

After requirements are collected and analysed at a reasonable amount, the next important activity is to prioritise the requirements based on business impact. As the digital solution leads, we need to develop criteria to prioritise the requirements based on factors depicted in the strategy and roadmap documents, as well as the financial and business priorities set by the sponsoring executives.

Following this methodical yet straightforward approach, we can be on top of issues and contribute to the control of cost. Reducing cost can also increase the financial viability of the digital solution. Besides we need to introduce innovation continuously, as a cost reduction enabler, as it can be the dominant player for overall cost management in complex digital environments. We cover the innovation in a separate chapter subsequently due to its significance in cost management and return on investment.

Chapter Summary and Take Away Points

Everything in enterprise transformation generates substantial cost. There are known and hidden costs.

Hidden costs are the more significant part of the proverbial iceberg.

We can contribute to reducing the solution costs by making trade-offs with a methodical and collaborative approach.

We increase the quality of the solutions by applying professional diligence, architectural rigour, delivery agility, smart collaboration across multiple teams, and harvesting re-usable materials.

Beware that there may be tremendous pressure from project managers and procurement staff to generate an upfront Bill of Materials due to demands of the project lifecycle. However, we can point out that without an approved architecture and design, we cannot commence purchasing materials.

There can be extensive infrastructure and maintenance costs associated with large data centres, server farms, mobile devices, storage units, data processing tools, analytics machines, and hosting in multi-Clouds.

Automated SLAs can detect low availability and poor performance. These automated SLAs trigger the rules and force the organisations breaching the agreements pay the contractually agreed penalties.

We need to pay attention to the SLAs from the nascent stages of the digital solution life cycle. The higher the quality of the solutions, the easier it is for SLAs to meet when the solutions are in production and the operational state. The rigour for quality in each phase can positively contribute to deal with SLA risks.

Some of the key considerations to address SLA issues could be autonomous condition monitoring and remote maintenance.

Digital transformations are long journeys moving the enterprises from chaos to coherence. The transformation process includes every aspect of the enterprise.

Enterprise digital systems can include business IT processes, business data, business applications, IT infrastructure, and IT service delivery. These domains can even be more complicated with the addition of geographical factors such as adding multiple countries to the equation.

One of the essential workaround solutions for dealing with this complexity is to modernise these primary domains iteratively in parallel.

The strategy document is a critical artefact to bring all parties and stakeholders on the same page. Then the digital solution leaders identify the critical dependencies among these domains based on the short term, midterm and long-term considerations.

A viability assessment must include key risks, constraints, and dependencies. The viability assessment can be the most informative tool a digital solution lead can provide to the sponsoring executives to make informed decisions.

As the digital solution leads, we need to develop criteria to prioritise the requirements based on factors depicted in the strategy and roadmap documents, as well as the financial and business priorities set by the sponsoring executives.

We need to introduce innovation continuously, as a cost reduction enabler, as it can be the dominant player for overall cost management in complex digital environments.

Chapter 6: Innovative & Inventive Intelligence

Purpose

I attempt to reflect upon my observations and thoughts on how digital leaders can use innovative and inventive intelligence coupled with collaborative principles of fusion-focused approach to initiate, empower, and deliver enterprise modernisation and transformation goals.

In this chapter, we aim to understand the importance of innovative and inventive intelligence as an empowering factor the success of digital modernisation and transformation. Let's reach a common understanding of the innovative and inventive thinking process in this practical context.

Innovation and Invention

We can define innovative and inventive thinking in different terms based on the type of work, professions, industry, and other backgrounds. In this book, my definition of innovative and inventive thinking is the use of creativity for generating novel ideas, new methods, new approaches, new techniques, new processes, and new tools or improve the current environment to gain insights, add compelling business value, reduce unnecessary costs, and increase desired revenue by focussing on return on investment.

Innovation and invention relate to novelty, improvement, iterations, and ongoing steady progress. Innovative and inventive thinking generates novel ideas, focuses on improving ideas, and strives for making continuous iterative progress. To this end, innovative and inventive thinking can use agile delivery principles to reach their goals. Innovative and inventive thinking can be practical.

Innovative and inventive thinking feeds the culture and is a critical aspect of a modernising digital ecosystem in transforming organisations. Enterprise cultures embracing innovative and inventive thinking approaches can naturally renew themselves to survive and thrive in fluctuating conditions, which are typical in modernising and transforming enterprises. These enterprises extend to the next generations with constant progress, renewed image, improved services, and stronger capabilities.

Innovation, inventions, technical excellence, and agility are interrelated. Innovative and inventive thinking ignites technical excellence, and technical excellence can be empowered by agility. Therefore, as digital leaders, we must be natural innovators and inventors producing results in agility. We need to practice innovative and inventive thinking in our daily life and motivate people around us. Now, let's attempt to find some practical ways to generate inventive and innovative intelligence.

Thinking Modes

Innovation and invention require multiple modes of thinking differently. Traditionally, most of us think vertically, linearly or in binary. We usually use vertical and linear types of thinking for problem-solving. Applying logic and streamlining thoughts are some techniques in this type of thinking mode. Linear thinking goes deep down, layer by layer, and in a logical manner. Binary thinking consists of simple terms such as yes or no, black and white, good or bad.

As opposed to vertical thinking, horizontal thinking covering more breadth rather than depth aims to generate unpredictable ideas by breaking out the rigid thought patterns. Horizontal thinking challenges the assumptions. This type of thinking looks for alternatives and goes beyond the ordinary, creating radical solutions.

We can apply horizontal thinking to create innovative and inventive ideas. There are different techniques that we can leverage horizontal thinking. Some commonly used techniques for horizontal thinking are randomisations, distortions, reversals, exaggerations, metaphors, analogies, dreaming, theme mining, questioning the norms, and creating contradictions.

One of the practical techniques to generate innovative and inventive ideas is to use mind mapping. We can articulate our thoughts using representative maps on paper or a whiteboard. We can also use other visual representations, such as drawing pictures on a whiteboard while explaining abstract ideas. People can visualise abstract ideas better by looking at the drawing as the proverbial a single picture can tell a thousand words.

Creating Innovation and Invention Culture

Many enterprises attempt to create an innovation and invention culture embedded in their modernising ecosystem. Digital leaders are the catalyst for the formation and maintenance of this empowering culture. With the support of their technical leaders, team members of these cultures continually challenge the status quo. People embrace changes and challenges in these cultures.

People collaborate better in cultures embracing innovative and inventive ideas. They see themselves with the changing conditions in new positions. They do not resist as they know that change can be useful for them. In these enriching cultures, they create excellence centres or ideation labs for people to try new ideas. They perform ongoing trials and errors to create and test their compelling ideas. They may fail at times, but they fail quickly and come back to reality with improved knowledge. They see the failing tests as new definitions.

Harnessing and driving creative thinking result in new cultures. As digital leaders, we need to cultivate the culture and inspire the team members. The best way for to ignite innovation and invention is to be a role model for our followers. We need to encourage the team members to innovate, invent and reward them for their achievements.

In modernising organisations, innovation and invention become habitual. Team members strive for excellence by creating new ideas in their day to day tasks. No one is called weird names or with other judgemental adjectives. Instead, new ideas are welcomed, praised, and even awarded in different ways. People embrace constant change and new ideas, even if they can be painful at times. They learn how to turn the pain to pleasure with the rewarding results of evident transformations.

Metaphorically, innovation is like air and water for our survival. In addition to survival, we need to use innovative and inventive thinking for thriving. We not only need to create innovations and inventions at a personal level but also through collaboration with the immediate teams and extended teams. We must keep asking how to deliver innovative and inventive experiences moment by moment continuously.

Design Thinking

One of the methods we can use is the design thinking activities which can take place daily in the team interactions. Design thinking allows the team to be intuitive and logical at the same time. Design thinking enables team members to be more creative to recognise new patterns. As design thinking is closely associated with the agile approach, the design thinking professionals progress their ideas iteratively. Enterprise modernisation initiatives require the adoption of design thinking to its core culture.

Growth Mindset

We need to have a growth mindset to ignite innovation and invention in the ecosystem. We must help our team members with a fixed mindset to convert to a growth mindset. As a growth mindset can lead to innovative and inventive solutions, it must be a build-in characteristic in the personalities of people in the digital ecosystem.

As intelligent digital leaders, we must lead to a mindset shift in small and large teams. We must hold a positive 'can do' attitude for any challenges we come across.

We must be customer-centric and put ourselves in customers' shoes with strong empathy. Using design thinking techniques, we can develop empathy maps. The mindset based on empathy is part of the design thinking practice.

Co-creation

To ignite innovation, we need to consider market conditions and the needs of clients. These conditions can help us generate new ideas. Listening to our clients carefully and collaborating with them can help us focus on innovative thinking. Many innovations can be co-created with clients.

A client-centric innovation and invention approach can be invaluable. We can link client concerns, requirements and aspirations to the organisation's capabilities then define the focus areas for innovation and invention agendas to enable digital transformation to address their needs.

Innovation and Invention Roadblocks

There can be many visible and invisible roadblocks to innovation; therefore, it is critical to recognise potential roadblocks. The roadblocks can be in various forms and from various angles. One of the main roadblocks is keeping the status quo. Traditional enterprises and business processes maintain the status quo. There is a strong resistance to change in these cultures.

Many organisations nowadays recognise the importance of innovative and inventive thinking.

However, there is always an unknown fear and resistance towards novelties by some people who may have hidden agendas.

As digital leaders, we must recognise those people who may try to sabotage innovative and inventive thinking in the modernisation programs. Even though these people with a negative mindset may be in the minority, they still can have a tremendous adverse impact on desired progress.

One way of dealing with resisting people is to be transparent to them and have a close face to face conversations. We must find ways to engage those types of people and show the value and benefit of new ideas to these types of people. If those people can see the value for themselves, then they can be converted to supporters. The critical point is asking them and making them think positively.

The business as usual mentality can be a roadblock for new ideas. Cumbersome business processes can be deterrent factors. More importantly, tired employees can hardly have any interest in innovation and inventions as they cannot see the immediate need. The best way is to separate new and old business as usual as two different departments. However, we must find some collaborative ways to bridge them.

Of course, business, as usual, is essential for the organisation to continue its current function but these organisations also need innovation and invention for transforming to the digital world with new insights, market competitiveness, and revenue generation. Modernisation and transformation programs must be kept separate from the business as usual practices to prevent any adverse effect of traditional thinking; however, we must integrate them in a way to prevent the undesirable effects of the old thinking models.

Chapter Summary and Take Away Points

Innovation and invention relate to novelty, improvement, iterations, and ongoing steady progress. Innovative and inventive thinking generates novel ideas, focuses on improving ideas, and strives for making continuous iterative progress.

Enterprise cultures embracing innovative and inventive thinking approaches can naturally renew themselves to survive and thrive in fluctuating conditions, which are typical in modernising and transforming enterprises.

Innovation, inventions, technical excellence, and agility are interrelated. Innovative and inventive thinking ignites technical excellence, and technical excellence can be empowered by agility.

We usually use vertical and linear types of thinking for problem-solving. Applying logic and streamlining thoughts are some techniques in this type of thinking mode.

Horizontal thinking covering more breadth rather than depth aims to generate unpredictable ideas by breaking out the rigid thought patterns. Horizontal thinking challenges the assumptions. This type of thinking looks for alternatives and goes beyond the ordinary, creating radical solutions.

Some commonly used techniques for horizontal thinking are randomisations, distortions, reversals, exaggerations, metaphors, analogies, dreaming, theme mining, questioning the norms, and creating contradictions.

One of the practical techniques to generate innovative and inventive ideas is to use mind mapping. We can articulate our thoughts using representative maps on paper or a whiteboard.

People collaborate better in cultures embracing innovative and inventive ideas. They see themselves with the changing conditions in new positions. They do not resist as they know that change can be useful for them.

The best way for to ignite innovation and invention is to be a role model for our followers. We need to encourage the team members to innovate, invent and reward them for their achievements.

In modernising organisations, innovation and invention become habitual. Team members strive for excellence by creating new ideas in their day to day tasks.

We not only need to create innovations and inventions at a personal level but also through collaboration with the immediate teams and extended teams.

Design thinking allows the team to be intuitive and logical at the same time. Design thinking enables team members to be more creative to recognise new patterns.

We need to have a growth mindset to ignite innovation and invention in the ecosystem. We must help our team members with a fixed mindset to convert to a growth mindset.

We must be customer-centric and put ourselves in customers' shoes with strong empathy. Using design thinking techniques, we can develop empathy maps. The mindset based on empathy is part of the design thinking practice.

We need to consider market conditions and the needs of clients. These conditions can help us generate new ideas. Listening to our clients carefully and collaborating with them can help us focus on innovative thinking. Many innovations can be co-created with clients.

There can be many visible and invisible roadblocks to innovation; therefore, it is critical to recognise potential roadblocks. The roadblocks can be in various forms and from various angles. One of the main roadblocks is keeping the status quo.

There is always an unknown fear and resistance towards novelties by some people who may have hidden agendas. We must recognise those people who may try to sabotage innovative and inventive thinking in the modernisation programs.

We must find ways to engage resisting people and show the value and benefit of new ideas to these types of people.

The business as usual mentality can be a roadblock for new ideas. Cumbersome business processes can be deterrent factors. More importantly, tired employees can hardly have any interest in innovation and inventions as they cannot see the immediate need.

Chapter 7: Smart Simplification

Purpose

We dedicated this chapter to simplicity; as mentioned previously, simplicity is a crucial pillar in our digital intelligence framework. Simplicity is a substantial requirement to be fulfilled for digital transformations and modernisation goals. Simplicity is also one of the critical attributes of digital leaders. Digital leaders must be capable of turning complexity to simplicity. Let's touch on the reasons briefly.

Reason for Simplicity

Simplicity touches almost every angle of modernisation solutions, as these solutions can incredibly complex. Simplicity, in sophisticated enterprises, is a paradoxical topic. Enterprise modernisation and transformations are complex tasks and require sophisticated intelligence such as in-depth knowledge, varied skills, and extensive experience. We must simplify the complicated processes, systems, tools and technologies using our digital intelligence.

Paradoxically, to create simplicity, one needs to deal with a lot of complexity, complications and sophisticated matters. This is where digital intelligence plays an important role. Obtaining the required knowledge, acquiring advanced skills, and gaining substantial experience are not easy and not indeed trivial activities. We need to deal with complexity using our digital intelligence to create simplicity.

From my observations, digitally intelligent leaders who deal with complexity and sophisticated matters can have extraordinary attributes to simplify things for other people. Creating simplicity requires effective communication.

Simplicity is a well sought-after characteristic in digital services and products. The modern digital world aims to offer simplified solutions to consumers. As opposed to complexity, simplicity is favourable by consumers. Therefore, digital leaders are expected to simplify complex situations and complicated problems and offer simple solutions. Communication simplicity is one of the critical factors; hence, we emphasise it in the next section.

Communication Simplicity

Digitally intelligent leaders are expected to articulate the most complicated and complex matters in a simple format that is understandable by others. Creating simplicity requires in-depth knowledge and flexible thinking. Simplicity requires clear communication. One way of clear communication is to customise our message to people's level and the right context we communicate.

Simplicity is a desired attribute for dealing with technical matters and building relationships. Digital leaders must communicate in simple terms. They need to simplify technical matters when dealing with technical issues. They must establish relationships that depict simplicity and efficiency in their actions.

User-Centric Simplicity

Simplicity requires to ask the question of how we can create products and services simple, intuitive, and human-centric. The consumer-oriented simplicity is a requirement for leading innovative teams in the modernisation initiatives. Digital leaders, with this capability, need to motivate their teams to think in simple terms when conveying their messages for complicated technical processes.

The path to digital modernisation and transformation begins with simplifying the systems, tools, technology, and process components at all levels and layers. One of the effective ways to this simplification is automating routine tasks and repetitive technology stacks. Automation can help standardise and simplify convoluted and repetitive tasks prone to human errors. Digital leaders, while delving into details in technology, they also need to focus on emerging needs by simplifying them in consumer terms.

In general, consumers keep complaining that technology creates complexity and make it difficult to understand concepts and objects in natural human language. For example, many consumers complain about the cumbersome documentation written in a convoluted language. They also show their disapproval for voluminous of documents for the use of a small technology device. They call it a waste.

Process Simplicity

There is a generational disconnect in dealing with process simplicity. The old generation used to read manuals to solve their computer problems. Software stacks used to come with large read-me files. However, the new generation works with technology intuitively. They hardly look at product manuals. If they are stuck, they would usually watch a YouTube video on how to do something or how to troubleshoot something. Instead of reading, they prefer watching a video. We need to be mindful of this dramatic cultural shift in consumer technologies.

We need to have a mission to simplify the business and technology processes and make them user-centric. This effort aims at efficiency and effectiveness of technology product and services leading to modernisation and digital transformations.

Technology simplification is another critical point. Technology is rapidly transforming towards service orientation. Most of the technology domains are provided based on services models. The most common technology trend is the Cloud services model. In the Cloud services model, everything is provided as services. For example, cloud service models can be infrastructure, platform, and software as a service. Indeed, many other technology stacks and processes such as data analytics and business processes can be offered as simplified services.

The sophisticated services model in the back office requires substantial amounts of simplification for users to take benefits of using complicated technologies. We can add value to the business by simplifying these services for the team members. We must inspire our team members to simplify everything by empathising with consumers. Simplification is an innovative process that digital leaders must lead as role models.

Simplicity and clarity are closely related. Especially in the technical services industry, providing a transparent experience to the technical team members can be very beneficial. Besides, making this transparent experience available to the end-user even more simplified and more explicit formats for the usage patterns can add additional value to the service provision goals.

An effective way of providing simplicity to the consumer is to think like the consumers. Digital leaders must keep focusing on the core tenets of simplifying products and services for the best possible user experience and satisfactory consumption merits.

Design Simplicity

Design simplicity is an essential factor to consider in digital modernisation and transformation goals. Design simplicity has a tremendous impact on the subsequent phases of the modernisation lifecycle, such as service delivery and support. The simpler the design, the more effective the delivery and service support can be.

Applying design thinking, combined with adopting agile methods for design, is one of the simplification approaches. Simplification is an enabler for agile service delivery. Agile methods strive for simplifications using an iterative approach. Progressing with iterations can be simpler than progressing with whole chunks.

By applying agile methods to the design phase, complicated requirements are simplified using simple use cases based on personas. Complex systems are deconstructed to smaller parts and dealt with simpler chunks. We can simplify system relationships with iterative flows. The simplifying focus is on smaller building blocks.

Most of the technology services nowadays are digitally offered using mobile devices such as tablets and smartphones. Mobile designs must focus on simplicity by removing clutter from screens due to the nature of small screen views. These types of designs must focus on only fundamentally essential objects. These activities are fundamental considerations for enterprise modernisation goals.

Designing complex systems also require simplifications through modular and service-oriented designs. Modularity and modular approaches to complex solutions are essential for simplification, modernisation, and digital transformation. One of the approaches for the modernisation goals can be a domain-based walkthrough of simplifying modules of IT infrastructure, applications, architecture, middleware, security, network, and data domains.

To elaborate on design simplification in the technology domain, let's take containers as an example. Containers break down monolithic interdependent architectures into manageable, and independent components. A container, as a loosely coupled system, is an entire runtime environment in a bundle. It includes dependencies, binaries, libraries, and configuration files. These new techniques and approaches help us simplify the design process.

Intelligent digital leaders must be conscious of simplicity for design. They need to run workshops to convey the message for the intuitive user-centric designs based on simplicity principles.

Specification Simplicity

Convoluted specifications also require simplification. For many years, time and energy spent on the system and user specification of software and hardware products and services were substantial. They cost an enormous amount of funds for the projects developing the specifications with many talented engineers, technical architects and other technical specialists. However, it became evident that the investment made on these convoluted specifications yielded in little gain than expected.

The digital trends, mobile culture and agile approaches made substantial changes in addressing the cumbersome specifications, especially concerning the users or consumers. The deep-down technical details for user specifications were found unnecessary. Agile methods proposed simplifications of cumbersome specifications delivering in user stories format.

User stories are simple templates, including the functionalities, capabilities, and specifications from users or consumers point of view. Developing and understanding the user stories consist of a single page can be much more comfortable and more effective than developing or reading hundreds of pages of specifications in traditional methods.

Simplicity for Technical Language

Simplicity is also essential for technical communication. Effective technical communication requires simplification. The simplification process for communication enables to facilitate understanding of issues, risks and dependencies effectively. Simplified communication is a challenging task, but we can apply it to our day-to-day interactions by using specific rules and techniques. Intelligent digital leaders can translate complex problems into clear messages that can be acted on, execute with simplicity and agility.

Refraining from convoluted phrases and instead, use of precise language and explicit statements are essential factors in simplifying communication. Even though digital leaders may have an extensive vocabulary and broad range of technical terms, particularly in-depth knowledge of technical matters, they need to be able to use simple language to pass their message to non-technical people's level. For example, they can use different terms and references while speaking to a manager, a secretary, an executive, a salesperson, and a technician. They can customise their message as needed.

While we can use advanced business terms to senior executives to articulate a point, we need to use deep technical terms to talk with engineers or technical specialists. This awareness, customisation, and flexibility in communication is a crucial characteristic of digital leaders.

The attention span for our generation is relatively low due to many technical disruptions in our lives. To this end, digital leaders must get the point quickly before losing the attention of people. For example, we may use lively words to illustrate a situation rather than using abstract terms.

Simplicity in written communication is essential too. People don't have much time and brainpower to understand intricate details in a technical document. The authors in enterprise modernisation initiatives must be sharp and to the point with clear statements. Short sentences are always preferable to improve readability.

The main benefit of simplification for oral and written communication is to pass the desired message effectively in the shortest possible time. It is beneficial to refrain from jargons, big words and complex sentence structures in oral and written communication.

Being able to articulate a situation in the simplest possible terms also can increase the confidence of the target person when dealing with digital leaders. This capability is essential for digital enterprise modernisation and transformation activities.

The right context in simplifying the language is also required. It is essential to balance qualitative and quantitative aspects while conveying a message to the audience. Digital leaders must be context-aware and deliver their message in the right context. Digital leaders need to strive to articulate the business value proposition to the business stakeholders rather than showing off their technical eminence detailing convoluted details.

Governance Simplicity

Simplicity for governance also matter. Complex and complicated governance processes and procedures can be a hurdle for enterprise modernisation and transformation initiatives. They can cause delays, confusions, rework and low performance for the modernisation goals. Therefore, it is critical to simplify governance framework, process and procedures for these initiatives.

We must be aware of the importance of governance and pay special attention to the required rigour. We cannot compromise the quality requirements in governing technology solutions. However, while having this rigour, we also need to have a balance for delivering the message in the simplest possible terms and making the processes for governance in the most effective ways.

Digital leaders must stay on top of technology trends and developments to govern them for modernisation. As part of their governance role, they need to ensure all technology practices adhere to regulatory standards in their industries.

Data Simplicity

Data simplification is a widely discussed topic in all modernising IT environments. One way of simplifying data is to clean data, remove duplications and errors. Reducing data sources and volumes when needed are also used to simplify data management processes.

However, there is a paradoxical situation to point out for data volumes as far as simplicity is concerned for modernisation. For example, more data is believed to create complexity; however, this is not true. It is just the opposite situation. Since we have more data to feed the systems, the systems can produce better output with rich data.

We can achieve data simplicity through the right data analysis, intelligence, powerful tools, and effective management strategies. In other words, when correctly and purposefully analysed, more data can add better intelligence for modernising and transforming the data platforms.

We need to understand the importance of data for modernising initiatives and use established techniques and evolving methods in data science. We can leverage the industry knowledge and focus on simplifying data collection, process, management, storage and analytics.

Besides, for enterprise modernisation and transformation purposes, the traditional data management methods cannot suffice; therefore, we need to consider Big Data management technologies, process and tools for this simplification process. One of the simplified Big Data trends in massive digital transformation and modernisation initiatives is the use of Cloud services for Big Data solutions. There is even a specific Big Data as a Service model.

Presentation Simplicity

We also need to simplify our presentations for effectiveness. There may be many presentations to different stakeholders for enterprise modernisation and transformation initiatives. Digital leaders present to multiple groups using PowerPoint slides and Visio images. We need to use these tools very carefully to maintain the focus of the audience and effectively convey critical messages.

Dead from PowerPoint is a famous statement depicting inefficiencies of presentations using an excessive number of slides. Being brief and concise in presentations is also an essential simplification method for effective communication. For example, we can simplify team presentations by cutting unnecessary, irrelevant details and using a concise number of slides focusing on necessary points when using a PowerPoint as a tool.

Another crucial consideration is focusing on conveying the intended central message rather than trying to impress the audience with sophisticated communication techniques. Endless discussions may cloud the essential message; therefore, it is critical to control the presentation process and focus sharply on the essential points in our presentations.

Intelligent digital leaders can provide simplified, clear and concise presentations without compromising the quality of content and effectiveness of the message. They also can encourage the team members to follow simplicity principles in their presentations and provide constant constructive feedback to maintain this simplicity culture.

Chapter Summary and Take Away Points

Simplicity touches almost every angle of modernisation solutions, as these solutions can incredibly complex. Simplicity, in sophisticated enterprises, is a paradoxical topic.

Paradoxically, to create simplicity, one needs to deal with a lot of complexity, complications and sophisticated matters.

Digitally intelligent leaders are expected to articulate the most complicated and complex matters in a simple format that is understandable by others.

One of the effective ways to this simplification is automating routine tasks and repetitive technology stacks. Automation can help standardise and simplify convoluted and repetitive tasks prone to human errors.

We need to have a mission to simplify the business and technology processes and make them user-centric.

The sophisticated services model in the back office requires substantial amounts of simplification for users to take benefits of using complicated technologies.

Simplicity and clarity are closely related. Especially in the technical services industry, providing a transparent experience to the technical team members can be very beneficial.

Design simplicity has a tremendous impact on the subsequent phases of the modernisation lifecycle, such as service delivery and support. The simpler the design, the more effective the delivery and service support can be.

Mobile designs must focus on simplicity by removing clutter from screens due to the nature of small screen views. These types of designs must focus on only fundamentally essential objects.

Modularity and modular approaches to complex solutions are essential for simplification, modernisation, and digital transformation. One of the approaches for the modernisation goals can be a domain-based walkthrough of simplifying modules of IT infrastructure, applications, architecture, middleware, security, network, and data domains.

Convoluted specifications also require simplification. For many years, time and energy spent on the system and user specification of software and hardware products and services were substantial.

User stories are simple templates, including the functionalities, capabilities, and specifications from users or consumers point of view.

The simplification process for communication enables to facilitate understanding of issues, risks and dependencies effectively.

Refraining from convoluted phrases and instead, use of precise language and explicit statements are essential factors in simplifying communication.

While we can use advanced business terms to senior executives to articulate a point, we need to use deep technical terms to talk with engineers or technical specialists. This awareness, customisation, and flexibility in communication is a crucial characteristic of digital leaders.

The attention span for our generation is relatively low due to many technical disruptions in our lives. To this end, digital leaders must get the point quickly before losing the attention of people.

While having this rigour, we also need to have a balance for delivering the message in the simplest possible terms and making the processes for governance in the most effective ways.

One way of simplifying data is to clean data, remove duplications and errors. Reducing data sources and volumes when needed are also used to simplify data management processes.

We can achieve data simplicity through the right data analysis, intelligence, powerful tools, and effective management strategies.

Dead from PowerPoint is a famous statement depicting inefficiencies of presentations using an excessive number of slides.

Chapter 8: Agile Intelligence

Purpose

Agility is another critical pillar in our digital intelligence framework. As digital leaders, in this era, we must be agile and think on our feet. This agility can help us to be influential, credible, competitive, and productive in our modernisation and transformation engagements. Our business teams and customers expect us to act in agility.

Agile Thinking

We must keep asking how we can make our IT footprint more intuitive, responsive, and nimble day today. This approach is a foundational requirement of our modernisation and transformation initiatives. Whist dealing with legacy IT footprint to understand it in an agile manner, we also need to have the vision of well-functioning solutions and put our energies on rapid-paced iterative modernisation and transformation initiatives.

It is impossible to undertake successful digital initiatives with old methods. As this became a reality, many organisations embraced agility and matured in delivering rapidly. Agility is a particular concern for modernisation and digital transformations as consumer demands are increasing based on fast-paced delivery requirements.

Speed to Market

Speed to market is one of the most fundamental requirements of businesses nowadays. We can generate revenues only by acting very quickly. To this end, agile approaches became the new norm in modernising enterprises. Products are expected to be released faster than they were in the past. Security updates and bug fixes are required more frequently.

Agility affects all aspects of the digital enterprise. Hence, we need to act, behave, and approach in agility to every aspect of the modernisation and digital transformation solutions.

Promoting Agile

There may be some resistance to agile approaches in some traditionally acting businesses. However, promoting agile to many stakeholders nowadays can be reasonably easy due to its nature and compelling reasons.

As a positive aspect, agile is a particular interest to the new generations as they grow with agility in all walks of life. However, the older generation still has a sentimental attachment to waterfall methods.

There appears to be some comfort zone created for using waterfall methods in general. Therefore, we need to find some creative ways to promote agile to those resisting it and particularly to older generations.

Quality Perceptions for Agile

There is a common perception that agile methods cut things short hence reduce the quality; however, this is not true. Some agile projects increase the quality due to iterative approaches and checking quality more frequently in every iterative milestone.

We must articulate the benefits and compelling reasons to use the agile approach, especially for modernisations leading to digital transformations. It is not feasible to wait and see the end of a gigantic digital transformation project. There are always many unknowns; hence, it is not possible to see the end product without experimentation and constant trial and errors in smaller scales for modernisation.

An agile approach allows the team members to test their ideas iteratively. If they fail, they fail quickly and cheaply without costing lots of funds to the initiatives. This business value needs to be understood well and needs to be embedded in the culture of the organisations striving for transformation goals. We can be the catalyst for conveying the message and making the necessary cultural adjustments effectively.

As digital leaders, we must be motivators and ignite agility in all digital enterprise initiatives. As we are technically capable and business-focused, we need to show the value and share their knowledge and views with team members and other stakeholders. We should also actively participate in agile scrums and provide ongoing feedback and support to the scrum teams.

Agile Roles for Digital Leaders

Agile methods require multiple roles. The most common ones are the scrum master and the product owner. As digital leaders, we can perform the role of the product owner in agile scrums. As product owners, we can set the acceptance criteria for the product in the allocated modernisation sprint. As a scrum master, we can provide day to day guidance on developing agile user stories, clearing backlogs, running stand-up meetings, and designing iterative solutions.

Accelerated Intelligence

Accelerated intelligence for digital requires developing quick mental models on how technology users interact with their solution in each iteration. For an agile approach to succeed, we need to be capable of clearing backlogs in the most efficient ways.

With our rapid action-oriented approach, we can clear the backlogs quickly and in priority orders. Furthermore, we can use rewards and recognise the high achievers' effort and contributions for clearing the backlogs in the most effective and innovative ways.

Our agile intelligence can add value to architecture and design too. In many organisations, due to valid reasons, developing architecture and designs create fear for the sponsors. The main reason for this is that architecture involves things that are hard to change later. However, this doesn't mean we cannot apply agile to architecture.

There is a massive trend to use agile methods for developing architectural and design solutions. To address the fear of architecture and designs, I introduce the term pragmatic architecture in fast-paced modernisations and transformation initiatives. The next section explains this.

Pragmatic Approach

As digital leaders, we must take a pragmatic approach to architecture development when engaged in enterprise modernisation and transformation programs. We know that predicting the future is very hard; therefore, creating an upfront paragon of architecture is not practical.

The notion of perfection equates to failure in fast-paced transformation programs. We cannot afford the use of monolithic waterfall methods for developing architectures and designs for many months and even years.

Taking extended times is not feasible in this digital age any more. Consumers expect product and services much quicker than old times. Our profitability depends on our speed to market. Therefore, a pragmatic approach to architecture and design is essential, especially for digital initiatives.

To this end, an iterative approach to architecture can be the most effective investment in the earlier stages of the digital transformation. We can see the architecture development like product development. The iterative method can speed up the architectural process and improve the quality based on the minimally viable product development approach.

Another way of the pragmatic approach is to use a single domain and apply the learnings to the next domains. This single domain approach is another iterative approach which can help us progress with confidence and well-managed risk profile.

Agile Development

After architecture and design, another big topic and concern in modernisation and transformation initiatives is software or application development. By using waterfall methods developing a software product used take months and years in the past. Again, consumers cannot wait this long any more. The solution is applying an agile approach to software development. Fortunately, agile methods are more suited to the development areas in modernisation initiatives.

There are many evolving agile methods to support different kinds of development processes. Fortunately, many software developers embrace agile methods. They can see the results much more quickly. Use of evolving methods such as DevOps is also prime considerations for enabling modernisation leading to substantial digital transformations. DevOps brings the software development and infrastructure support operations teams together in an integrated way.

As digital leaders, we must encourage rapid application development and deployment of flexible solutions using appropriate agile methods in the organisation. We need to be mindful that speedy time-to-market for digital products is a competitive differentiator in this day and age. The rapid solutions to market can also delight our clients and increase their confidence in our products and services.

Automation and Standardisation

Modernisation goals leading to transforming to digital services and delivering products fast to market requires substantial automation and standardisation activities. Agile methods have a particular focus on automation and standardisation. Both automation and standardisation enable simplifying and speeding up processes.

As we understand the value of automation and standardisation for increasing the quality of our products and services, we need to encourage our teams to leverage these two enablers in our digital transformation solutions. Many teams would embrace both automation and standardisation as the value is quite clear and compelling.

Applying automation and standardisation to our digital transformation objectives, we can reduce the number of resources required to maintain manual and tedious tasks. Automation and standardisation can address human errors and resolve potential errors quickly. Enterprises embracing agile cultures do not resist automation and standardisation; in fact, they leverage the capabilities for modernisation and transformation goals.

By encouraging architects, designers and technical specialists to automate and standardise as much as possible, we can enable these valuable resources to participate in more value-adding roles rather than performing repetitive and boring tasks that computers can undertake. Team members focusing on stimulating and high-value items also tend to create more innovative solutions to empower enterprise modernisation and transformation progress.

Breaking Silos

Agile intelligence requires removing silos in enterprises. What I mean by silos are having isolated departments and teams without being integrated into other relevant departments and teams in the organisation. This separation is undesirable and can be unproductive.

Silos are proven to slow the whole enterprise modernisation and transformation lifecycle, including architecture, design, development, marketing, and selling products and services.

A siloed culture can also impact the quality of the products due to a lack of integrated views. Enterprise departments in silos may not know each other's progress and cause some duplicate of works or rework. They may not produce a single integrated product or services to the consumers.

Another undesirable implication of having silos is that some departments in these traditional settings in the same organisations even compete with each other. Internal competition is the worst enemy which can destroy any digital transformation goals and objectives.

Leveraging our agile intelligence, we can move from silos to a flatter structure to resolve the issues of isolated and hierarchical structures in large organisations. By leveraging the agile principles, we can pay special attention to collaboration, co-locations, and face to face teamwork rather than having silos and hierarchies in our organisations, leading to digital transformations.

As agile oriented digital leaders, we continuously need to deal with culture and modernising ecosystem implications. We can break silos, instead of coming above, we create flat structures, resulting in collaborative self-managing teams with many domain experts as peers.

Backlog Prioritisation

Digital transformation initiatives can have gigantic backlogs. Dealing with transformation backlogs can be very challenging. However, our speed-oriented intelligence serves well in clearing backlogs efficiently. Maintaining backlogs in agile methods can be systemic. As digital leaders in scrums, we can make day to day management of backlogs, in priority order, a habit.

Even if we perform the role of a scrum master or a product owner, as digital leaders, we need to keep the team members accountable for their backlog items. We can help the team manage their assigned backlogs items effectively.

Due to the importance of prioritisation, as digital leaders, we continuously must focus on the priority items and deal with the backlog items based on priority orders. Leveraging this priority approach and encouraging our team members, our team backlogs can run very efficiently and productively. We know that backlog management is a critical factor in digital transformation sprints.

Minimum Viable Product

One of the critical aspects of agile intelligence is the creation of a minimum viable product using agile principles. A sprint is the shortest time bombed duration to create the minimum viable product. Consumer expectations, financial constraints, resource issues, and business priorities all have an impact on setting priorities for clearing backlogs to create minimum viable products for our consumers. This agile principle can help us set the priorities for value creation for our business and clients.

Dealing with Constant Change

Agile intelligence mandate dealing with constant change. Change management is a vital aspect of enterprise modernisation and transformation initiatives. For the entire team, embracing change is critical to be successful in agile digital delivery. Adapting to constant change can be a valuable digital intelligence characteristic.

Managing every user story, clearing a backlog item on a timely basis, and running a sprint is all about constant change. Dealing with this constant change requires flexibility and agility in designing, developing and implementing agile solutions.

To this end, digital leaders and their team members engaged in agile processes and solutions adapt to the constant change. They become the change agents. Enterprise modernisation and transformation initiatives certainly need such a change-oriented agile intelligence.

Fail Rapidly, Early, and Cheaply

As we keep highlighting, one of the benefits of using agile approach comes from moving in small steps quickly. In other words, we tackle solutions in smaller chunks with agility. Agile methods enable the principles of the fail fast, fail early, fail cheaply. These principles are fundamental success factors for modernisation and digital transformation goals.

Of course, we don't fail for the sake of failure. No one enjoys failure, but it is beneficial to fail earlier than later to keep the cost of failure low and be successful in the long run using the lessons learnt from smaller failures. Learning from failures and redefining success is a crucial agile intelligence attribute for digital leaders.

Even though it is called 'fail fast' it refers to ongoing experimentation with constant trial and errors leading to further intelligence and learning to deal with unknowns in a fast and effective way. Learnings from these experimentations constitute desired progress for designing, developing and implementing complex solutions for enterprise modernisation and transformation goals.

Agile Cost Management

Agile intelligence also mandates cost awareness. In business, we can consider every resource and effort as a cost. Even though we, as digital leaders, are well paid and costing business for our salaries, as we are cost-aware and know how to reduce cost with our intelligent decisions, we make our projects profitable, generate more revenue, especially delivering rapidly. We focus on increasing efficiencies and lowering costs as part of our digital strategy.

Agile is a cost-focused and revenue-generating approach. We can manage costs better and generate more revenue by adopting agile principles in high impact tasks and solution development activities in modernisation and transformation solutions. Through incremental progress, prioritised backlog management, speedy iterative delivery through sprints, we can prevent the cost of failure for big chunks of work items and more importantly, we can turn the costs into revenues.

As agile digital leaders, we are capable of turning costs to investment. With a strong vision, innovative approaches, and agile delivery capabilities, the costs incurred from our initiatives can be an investment rather than cost. Most of the sponsoring executives understand that investment on visionary and well-performing digital leaders like us can generate new businesses and bring substantial revenues in modernisation and transformation initiatives with our contributions both at tactical and strategic levels.

Chapter Summary and Take Away Points

Speed to market is one of the most fundamental requirements of businesses nowadays. We can generate revenues only by acting very quickly.

An agile approach allows the team members to test their ideas iteratively. If they fail, they fail quickly and cheaply without costing lots of funds to the initiatives.

Agile methods require multiple roles. The most common ones are the scrum master and the product owner.

Accelerated intelligence for digital requires developing quick mental models on how technology users interact with their solution in each iteration.

The notion of perfection equates to failure in fast-paced transformation programs.

Taking extended times is not feasible in this digital age any more. Consumers expect product and services much quicker than old times. Our profitability depends on our speed to market.

Use of evolving methods such as DevOps is also prime considerations for enabling modernisation leading to substantial digital transformations. DevOps brings the software development and infrastructure support operations teams together in an integrated way.

Applying automation and standardisation to our digital transformation objectives, we can reduce the number of resources required to maintain manual and tedious tasks.

Automation and standardisation can address human errors and resolve potential errors quickly. Enterprises embracing agile cultures do not resist automation and standardisation; in fact, they leverage the capabilities for modernisation and transformation goals.

Silos are proven to slow the whole enterprise modernisation and transformation lifecycle.

By leveraging the agile principles, we can pay special attention to collaboration, co-locations, and face to face teamwork rather than having silos and hierarchies in our organisations.

We continuously must focus on the priority items and deal with the backlog items based on priority orders.

One of the critical aspects of agile intelligence is the creation of a minimum viable product using agile principles.

Managing every user story, clearing a backlog item on a timely basis, and running a sprint is all about constant change.

Agile methods enable the principles of the fail fast, fail early, fail cheaply. These principles are fundamental success factors for modernisation and digital transformation goals.

Agile is a cost-focused and revenue-generating approach. As agile digital leaders, we are capable of turning costs to investment.

Chapter 9: Collaborative Intelligence

Purpose

As digital leaders, we certainly need to take leverage of collaborative intelligence. It is inevitable. In this section, we cover the importance of useful terms fusion and collaboration from a productivity angle in the modernising and transforming enterprise. Let's understand the meaning of collaboration in our desired context.

Meaning of Collaboration

We know that the term collaboration is overused and loses its significance, especially with the emergence of internet technologies. People keep saying collaborative or collaboration tools, especially in a social media context.

In its true meaning, collaboration refers to a team of people working together for mutual goals to achieve successful and synergetic outcomes. The team, mutual goals and synergetic outcomes are essential entities of this simple framework. Our focus is, of course, on the work aspect of the collaboration rather than entertainment or hobbies.

Collaboration may take place in different modes and formats. One example is two or more people sharing ideas for a project plan. At a basic level, people may also collaborate by writing using various documentation tools such as Box, Google docs, or network version of Microsoft Office products. There are also emerging tools mainly used in mobile settings. These mobility tools are widespread in agile methods. To give an idea, some of these tools are Slack, Trello, Twitter, Facebook Messenger, and many more.

Most of us tout social media tools as practical, useful, and highly valuable for collaboration purposes. However, when we carefully examine these tools, we can see that they are more information-sharing tools rather than actual collaboration tools. From my experience, the most productive and impactful collaboration tools are face to face meetings, telephone, and video conferencing.

Collaboration is an essential intelligence type for digital leaders to create outstanding results using synergy. As digital leaders, we collaborate widely and productively. We also motivate our team members to collaborate effectively and efficiently by pointing out the common goals and making them compelling for collaboration. Now let's discuss fusion.

Fusion

We can consider fusion an empowering intelligence for digital leaders. The term fusion refers to joining different things with different attributes or functions together to create a single new entity or form. The notion of fusion relates to concepts such as integration, blending, merging, amalgamation, synergy, and bonding.

Fusion is closely related to collaboration from several angles. Fusion is a type of collaboration designed for specific and advanced missions. Fusion principles suit the goals of digital progress in an enterprise.

Fusion principles aim to bring individuals from various backgrounds, small groups with different purposes, various teams with differing capabilities, communities of practices with different missions under a single umbrella for serving a joint mission.

Fusion is the most advanced and effective type of collaboration especially required for complex and complicated modernisation initiatives with unique goals and market focus. Creating fusion-based collaboration can be very challenging. As digital leaders, with extensive technical and people skills and experiences, we can create fusion-based collaboration.

Fusion can also refer to integrating old systems, tools, and processes and creating new systems. This transformative approach is a critical factor for enterprise modernisation and transformation goals. From an awareness perspective, we need to understand the significance of fusion principles and apply them to help our organisations to modernise the enterprise effectively.

There are different ways to enable fusion in an organisation. As digital leaders, we usually take responsibility to initiate fusion in our immediate and extended teams.

We must be passionate about achieving our digital goals using fusion principles. We don't wait for fusion to happen by itself. We know that nothing can happen by itself. Naturally, someone with leadership and architectural skills must initiate it. This action-oriented focus on fusion is one of the outstanding characteristics of strategic leaders, who are typically extrovert people.

Once we initiate fusion and invite our collaborators to structured activities, then the process is maintained with necessary communication and engagement rules. Effective communication is a critical enabler of fusion goals. Depending on the medium, both verbal and written communication types are essential for fusion to happen.

Fusion for co-located teams are usually conducted on face to face and can primarily be dynamic in delivery. However, geographically distant teams usually use video conferencing, telephone, chat programs, email or some agile collaboration tools.

In remote teams, written communication is critical. Written communications can create some challenges, such as a careless piece of writing may cause some offence and kill the spirit of collaboration. Therefore, as digital leaders, we play an essential role in facilitating these types of communication by moderating communication channels delicately.

After we initiate and enable fusion goals, we need to maintain the desired outcomes. We can create the necessary process and procedures to maintain collaborative activities. Effective use of our strategic leadership skills is mandatory to achieve fusion goals in modernisation and transformation initiatives.

Even though we set the initial team and processes to support the team activities, it is also the responsibilities of other team members to contribute to the goals set by our collaborative plans. To this end, as digital leaders, we also take the role of motivators to keep the team inspired by showing their impactful vision and strategic goals.

By focusing on productive fusion at various levels, we leverage insights from cross-functional teams and community of practices to create differentiated value propositions for the modernisation goals.

By undertaking many tasks to initiate and maintain fusion, we keep repeating these activities multiple times with multiple teams and integrate these teams to aggregate more intensive collaboration. The magic of fusion starts with these repetitions.

Successful repetitions make ripple effects for more success. In a relatively short time frame, these teams can create a collaborative culture based on fusion principles aligned with the organisation's ecosystem and strategic goals.

This collaborative culture at work can be invaluable. When collaborative culture starts flourishing using fusion-based collaboration, a desirable phenomenon called innovation happens naturally. Collaboration and innovation are tightly coupled processes, as we mentioned in previous chapters. Now, let's discuss diversity within collaboration and fusion context.

Diversity

The power of connected people from diverse backgrounds for the same goal generates new ideas and insights. Some of these ideas and insights may touch people from different angles and further motivate them even to take more responsibilities in this transforming ecosystem.

With the ignition of the initial strategic technical leadership, this shift causes the emergence of new technical leaders in modernising enterprises. Innovation generates collaborative culture and can be highly desirable for creating new business and growing established businesses by modernising the enterprise leading to desired digital transformation goals. Innovation is one of the exciting results provided by a collaborative culture with diversity, inclusiveness and implementation of fusion approach.

This magical aspect of fusion and collaboration leading to innovation is an ideal situation for transforming the enterprise. As digital leaders, we must take advantage of this desirable situation by creating, maintaining, facilitating and further improving the situations.

Collaborative Influence

Digital intelligence helps us influence our team members to collaborate more effectively. Influence is an essential strategic leadership attribute. It is particularly essential to create a collaborative culture in transforming and modernising environments. As digital leaders, we influence our collaborators by demonstrating responsibility, accountability, and credibility.

Credibility

Credibility in dynamic environments can be critical. In other words, as digital leaders responsible for transforming environments, we must be credible. Promoting change in these dynamic environment sand obtaining buy-in for transforming from other people require credibility.

As digital leaders, we can earn the trust of our collaborators with credibility and integrity. Our vision, strategy, knowledge, skills, actions have an impact on our credibility. Our goals and our organisations' goals must align with these critical attributes.

Consistency and predictability for our behaviour are critical factors for credibility. To survive, thrive and succeed for our goals, we must pay special attention to remain credible at all times in our fields.

Trust and Collaborative Engagement

When we establish trust, another magic happens. People start sharing their true selves. They become more productive and more creative. A collaborative culture is an empowering contributor and enabler of modernising enterprises.

Digital intelligence requires people from diverse background to engage in collaborative activities. Enabling diversity is a critical factor in creating collaborative teams and inclusive cultures. Diversity is extra critical for modernisation and transformation goals due to the required creativity and innovation by people from different backgrounds, skills sets, and experiences.

We can establish diversity with trust. Let's keep in mind that only with trust and trusted environments, people can show their true identities. When people start showing their true self, a diverse culture starts flourishing. Diversity is an enhancer of collaboration and fusion.

More importantly, with diversity, also innovation come to the picture. We can notice it stronger and faster. Diverse ideas ignite and accelerate innovation. With this approach, we can create new options and choices. Connecting those choices and options also make a ripple effect on the culture. With this understanding, we can conclude that trust-based diversity can be a valuable contributor to modernisation programs.

Chapter Summary and Take Away Points

In its true meaning, collaboration refers to a team of people working together for mutual goals to achieve successful and synergetic outcomes.

The term fusion refers to joining different things with different attributes or functions together to create a single new entity or form. The notion of fusion relates to concepts such as integration, blending, merging, amalgamation, synergy, and bonding.

Fusion is the most advanced and effective type of collaboration especially required for complex and complicated modernisation initiatives with unique goals and market focus. Creating fusion-based collaboration can be very challenging.

Effective communication is a critical enabler of fusion goals. Depending on the medium, both verbal and written communication types are essential for fusion to happen.

The power of connected people from diverse backgrounds for the same goal generates new ideas and insights. Some of these ideas and insights may touch people from different angles and further motivate them even to take more responsibilities in this transforming ecosystem.

This magical aspect of fusion and collaboration leading to innovation is an ideal situation for transforming the enterprise.

As digital leaders, we influence our collaborators by demonstrating responsibility, accountability, and credibility.

We can earn the trust of our collaborators with credibility and integrity.

Consistency and predictability for our behaviour are critical factors for credibility.

We can establish diversity with trust. When people start showing their true self, a diverse culture starts flourishing. Diversity is an enhancer of collaboration and fusion.

Chapter 10: Technology Intelligence

Purpose

In this section, we cover the prominent technologies and briefly introduce them by highlighting their importance for modernisation and digital transformation goals. Instead of delving into details and providing an exhaustive list, our focus is only on foundational technologies which can make a real difference. Let's touch on the critical technologies and technical skills that digital leaders need to possess for leading successful modernisation and transformation initiatives.

Technology intelligence is a mandatory attribute for digital leaders. We must be up-to-date with digital technologies and possess a wide range of vital technical knowledge and skills. There are many growing and emerging technologies that we need to be conversant. As digital leaders, we must focus on using emerging technologies as enablers of the enterprise modernisation and transformation goals.

Enabling Technologies

The key technology enablers of enterprise modernisation and transformation goals are Cloud Computing, Mobile technologies, IoT, Big Data, and Data Analytics. An integrated view of these technologies, associated processes and tools are critical to success in our digital endeavours. Besides, we must focus on benchmarking of technological products and services as they are essential enablers of digital transformations.

Cloud

Nowadays, the most widely used technology in transforming enterprises is Cloud Computing. Cloud became mainstream in many organisations. Adaptation of Cloud became very rapid. We can use Cloud as a foundational enterprise modernisation and transformation tool.

The most significant attribute of Cloud is that the cloud service model can expand or reduce computer resources based on service requirements. For example, Cloud can provide the maximum resources when we need a large amount of computing power, storage capacity, or network bandwidth for a specific workload at a particular timeframe. Then we can release these resources after completing our specific mission for these workloads. This elasticity and scalability of Cloud can provide value position for digital transformations.

'Pay per use' or 'pay as you go' is another essential characteristic that Cloud services model provides. The resources can be consumed based on the usage amount. Usage could be a short- or long-term basis.

For example, consumers can pay based on computing power or storage amount they used. Related to 'pay per use', using 'on-demand' is another characteristic of the Cloud services model. Consumers can use when they demand the required services without upfront payment or dedicated investment for the IT resources in their organisation.

The recent commercial trend for using virtual machines in publicly available Cloud services are based on three types of instances such as on-demand instance, reserved instance and spot instance. In on-demand instance, there is no long-term commitment. Reserved instance is a relatively longer-term with a substantial discount compared to on-demand usage. For the spot instance, as commonly promoted several service providers, the price is agreed based on bidding.

Cloud offers resiliency to the infrastructure, applications and services. System failures such as servers or storage units can be automatically isolated with predefined instructions, and workloads are migrated to redundant virtual units without disrupting the service levels or consumer usage. Cloud's resilience attribute removes many of our supportability concerns in our solution requirements.

Based on consumer requirements, Cloud resources can be virtual or physical. This flexibility is created by multitenancy characteristic of the Cloud service model. For example, a Cloud service provider can host multiple user workloads in the same infrastructure without adversely affecting their privacy and security. If there are high-security requirements such as sensitive governmental services, isolation can be physical. We need to consider constraints and limitations which can affect the use of virtual services in multi-tenancy mode.

Flexible workload movement is another crucial attribute of Cloud service model. There may be times an organisation requires to run their workloads in a different time zone, and the workloads can easily be moved to a data centre in another country. This requirement may be for several reasons such as reducing cost, providing a better service for a focus group in a different location or even regulatory requirements. Let's introduce the next important technology, which is proliferating globally.

IoT

After Cloud, another emerging technology is the IoT (Internet of Things). As digital leaders, we need to understand this vital technology. Substantial progress has been made in many disciplines owing to the use of IoT in creating new services and products. Some of these disciplines include environmental monitoring, manufacturing, infrastructure management, energy management, agriculture, healthcare, transportation, IT, electronics, material sciences and banking.

In the market, it is noticeable that IoT technologies are emerging and IoT solutions are growing exponentially. Some organisations estimate billions of devices in the next few years to connect to the global IoT ecosystem. The bottom line is that IoT is valuable for both business and economy, which is inevitable. From our current experience, we can construe that IoT can have a substantial impact on our economy and the way we do business and commerce.

Consumers and service providers have an incredible interest and focus on this fantastic technology powered by the internet. The generation of new business for companies and new job roles that we cannot even name yet is imminent. Some believe that the IoT can be as important as the emergence of the internet itself. Some even point out that it can be the next big thing in our lives. These are, of course, speculations, combined with some media hype; however, time can tell as to whether the high expectations of IoT to be met. As digital leaders, we need to understand IoT offerings and possess a broad range of IoT knowledge and skills because IoT is one of the primary enablers of the modernisation and digital transformation initiatives to create new revenue streams.

Big Data and Analytics

In addition to IoT, Big Data and Analytics are vital technologies and processes that we need to understand. Not only understand, but also, we must use them for creating insights and competitive advantage for our organisations.

It is important to note that even though architecturally similar to traditional data, Big Data requires newer methods and tools to deal with data. The traditional methods and tools are not adequate to process big data.

The Big Data process refers to capturing a substantial amount of data from multiple sources, storing analysing, searching, transferring, sharing, updating, visualising and governing huge volumes data such as petabytes or even exabytes.

Interestingly, the main concern or aim of Big Data is not the amount of data but more advanced analytics techniques to produce value out of these large volumes of data. The advanced analytics in this context refers to approaches such as descriptive, predictive, prescriptive, and diagnostic analytics.

We need to understand the type of analytics and when to use them for what type of solutions. The descriptive analytics deals with situations such as what is happening right now based on incoming data. The predictive analytics refers to what might happen in the future. Prescriptive analytics deals with actions to be taken. Diagnostic analytics ask the question of why something happened. Each analytics type serves difference scenarios and use-cases.

Big Data Analytics is a comprehensive business-driven discipline. At a high level, it aims to make quick business decisions, reduce the cost for a product or service, and test new market to create new products and services. All industries nowadays use Big Data analytics. For example, health care, life sciences, manufacturing, government, and retail are extensively using Big Data and Analytics.

We need new methods and tools to perform Big Data analytics. There are emerging methods and many tools available on the market. Most of the methods are proprietary, but some are available via open-source programs. Some popular tools frequently mentioned in the Big Data Analytics publications are Aqua Data Studio, Azure HDinsight, IBM SPSS Modeler, Skytree, Talend, Splice Machine, Plotly, Lumify, Elasticsearch.

Besides, open-source has progressed well in this area and produced multiple powerful tools. Some commonly used open-source analytics tools are Apache Hadoop, Apache Spark, Apache Storm, Apache Cassandra, Apache SAMOA, Neo4j, MongoDB, and R programming environment.

These tools are beyond our scope, but it is useful to create awareness as they are widely used in digital transformation.

Big Data analytics is a broad and growing area. We can better understand Big data analytics looking at its inherent characteristics. We can summarise these characteristics using the following terms connection, conversion, cognition, configuration, content, customisation, cloud, cyber, and community.

As these terms are self-explanatory, we don't need to go into details to explain each here. We also need to familiarise ourselves with Big Data analytics methods and techniques. Some of these methods and techniques are natural language processing, data mining, association pattern mining, behavioural analytics, predictive analytics, descriptive analytics, prescriptive analytics, diagnostic analytics, and machine learning.

Machine learning is a trending discipline. It is widely adopted. Machine learning refers to computer systems to learn and improve based on their learning from the analysis of large volumes of data sets without programming. It is part of the artificial intelligence domain in computer science. Due to its usefulness and impact, machine learning became a vital technology and tool for enterprise modernisation strategies leading to digital transformation.

Related to machine learning, we also need to understand unstructured data handling, particularly text analytics. Text analytics include machine learning, computational linguistics, and traditional statistical analysis. Text analytics focus on converting massive volumes of a machine or human-generated text into meaningful structures to create business insights and support decision-making.

There are various text analytics techniques that we need to familiarise. For example, information extraction is one of the text analytics techniques which extract structured data from unstructured text.

Text summarisation is another widely used unstructured data processing technique which can automatically create a condensed summary of a document or selected groups of documents. We can use text summarization technique, especially for blogs, news, product documents, and scientific papers.

Natural Language Processing (NLP) is another sophisticated text analytics technique interfaced as question and answers in natural language. NLP is commonly used in various commercial products such as Siri by Apple, Watson by IBM, and Alexa by Amazon products.

Cybersecurity

In addition to analytics, security is the next critical knowledge and skill that we must possess. Particular security which we call cybersecurity is even more critical. Cybersecurity touches every aspect of enterprise modernisation and transformation initiatives. Cybersecurity is a vast security domain covering every aspect of security management, such as identity and access management, authentication, authorisation, encryption, and many more areas. Application of cybersecurity is a critical enabler for securing modernisation and digital transformation solutions.

Cloud Computing, IoT and Big Data also mandate cybersecurity at all levels. Broader security awareness and associated skills are essential for digital initiatives.

Related to advanced security, Blockchain, which is relatively new technology, is becoming critical for new security requirements which could be enablers for modernisation goals.

Network

As digital leaders, we deal with the network all the time. Enterprise modernisation and transformation solutions touch every aspect of networking such as wide area, local area, wireless and many more networking types. Networks are enablers of Cloud, IoT, Blockchain, and Big Data analytics.

Since the network and associated communication technologies are the fundamental enablers of enterprise modernisation goals, understanding functions of network and network implications such as security, latency, bandwidth, are also important topics that technology leaders need to cover broadly and in-depth based on their involvement.

Mobility

Mobility is a critical interrelated technology domain in organisations moving to mobile solutions hence we need to understand and educate our teams for the effective use of mobility for innovations leading to business insights and collaboration across the organisation including the customers and partners.

We also need to understand the domain of Enterprise Mobile Management. This domain includes essential components such as device management, application management, content management, email management, and unified endpoint management.

Mobility is associated with several architectural and business considerations such as network access, compliance, data management, workplace demographics, end-user accountability and BYOD (Bring Your Own Devices) concepts.

IT Service Management

IT service management is inevitable for transforming enterprises. IT service management covers an extensive array of technology, process, and tools. IT service management includes processes such as change management, problem management, incident management, service level management, capacity management, availability management, business continuity management, and security management.

In addition, system management processes such as monitoring, alerting and event management can be covered under the umbrella term of IT Service Management. These processes are managed using many technological tools. More importantly, these tools need to be architected, integrated, designed and implemented coherently for enterprise digital transformation goals.

Understanding the dynamics of these tools within the context of modernisation initiatives are vital for successful outcomes. One of the best representations of IT Service model is implemented using popular ITIL (Information Technology Infrastructure Library. Knowledge of ITIL can be handy in communicating our service management needs to broader stakeholders in the enterprise.

Chapter Summary and Take Away Points

The key technology enablers of enterprise modernisation and transformation goals are Cloud Computing, Mobile technologies, IoT, Big Data, and Data Analytics.

The most significant attribute of Cloud is that the cloud service model can expand or reduce computer resources based on service requirements.

Flexible workload movement is another crucial attribute of Cloud service model. There may be times an organisation requires to run their workloads in a different time zone, and the workloads can easily be moved to a data centre in another country.

In the market, it is noticeable that IoT technologies are emerging and IoT solutions are growing exponentially.

Consumers and service providers have an incredible interest and focus on IoT powered by the internet.

Big Data and Analytics are vital technologies and processes that we need to understand.

The Big Data process refers to capturing a substantial amount of data from multiple sources, storing analysing, searching, transferring, sharing, updating, visualising and governing huge volumes data such as petabytes or even exabytes.

Big Data analytics is a broad and growing area. We can better understand Big data analytics looking at its inherent characteristics. They are connection, conversion, cognition, configuration, content, customisation, cloud, cyber, and community.

Machine learning is a trending discipline. It is widely adopted. Machine learning refers to computer systems to learn and improve based on their learning from the analysis of large volumes of data sets without programming.

Text analytics include machine learning, computational linguistics, and traditional statistical analysis. Text analytics focus on converting massive volumes of a machine or human-generated text into meaningful structures to create business insights and support decision-making.

NLP is commonly used in various commercial products such as Siri by Apple, Watson by IBM, and Alexa by Amazon products.

Cybersecurity is a vast security domain covering every aspect of security management, such as identity and access management, authentication, authorisation, encryption, and many more areas.

Since the network and associated communication technologies are the fundamental enablers of enterprise modernisation goals, understanding functions of network and network implications such as security, latency, bandwidth, are also important topics.

Mobility is associated with several architectural and business considerations such as network access, compliance, data management, workplace demographics, end-user accountability and BYOD concepts.

IT service management includes processes such as change, problem, incident, service level, capacity, availability, business continuity, and security management.

Knowledge of ITIL can be handy in communicating our service management needs to broader stakeholders in the enterprise.

Chapter 11: Data Intelligence

Purpose

Data is the most valuable asset in business intelligence. Data steers and leads to business intelligence. One significant fact is that data, especially Big Data, is ubiquitous in every enterprise. Every enterprise generates massive amounts of data. As digital leaders, data is our bread and butter; hence, we need to understand every aspect of it in its lifecycle. Let's start with Big Data.

Big Data

Big data is different from traditional data. The main differences come from characteristics such as volume, velocity, variety, veracity, value and overall complexity of data sets in a data ecosystem.

Volume refers to the size or amount of data sets. We can measure them in terabytes, petabytes or exabytes. There are no specific definitions to determine the threshold for Big Data volumes. Ironically, even though it is called the Big Data, and it is a signifier, the volume is not the main characteristics of the Big Data as far as architecture, design and deployments are concerned.

Velocity refers to the speed of producing data. Big Data sources generate high-speed data streams coming from real-time devices such as mobile phones, social media, IoT sensors, IoT edge gateways, and the Cloud data stores. Velocity is an essential factor in all phases of the Big Data architecture and management considerations.

Variety refers to multiple sources of data. The data sources include structured transactional data, semi-structured such as web sites or system logs, and unstructured data such as video, audio, animation, and pictures. Variety is also a significant factor for Big Data architecture and management considerations.

Veracity means the quality of the data. Since volume and velocity are enormous in Big Data, veracity is very challenging. It is essential to have quality output to make sense of data for business insights. Veracity is also related to value.

Value is the primary purpose of Big Data to create new insights and gain business value from Big Data. We can create value with innovative and creative approaches taken by all the stakeholders of a Big Data solution.

Overall complexity for Big Data refers to more data attributes and difficulty to extract desired value due to large volume, wide variety, enormous velocity and required veracity for the desired value.

More on Big Data

Even though architecturally similar to traditional data, Big Data requires newer methods and tools to deal with data. The traditional methods and tools are not adequate to process Big Data. The process refers to capturing a substantial amount of data from multiple sources, storing analysing, searching, transferring, sharing, updating, visualising and governing huge volumes data in the magnitude of petabytes or even exabytes.

The main concern or aim of Big Data is not the amount of data but more advanced analytics techniques to produce value out of these large volumes of data. The advanced analytics in this context refers to approaches such as descriptive, predictive, prescriptive, and diagnostic analytics.

The descriptive analytics deals with situations such as what is happening right now based on incoming data. The predictive analytics refers to what might happen in the future. Prescriptive analytics deals with actions to be taken. Diagnostic analytics ask the question of why something happened. Each analytics type serves difference scenarios and use-cases. Now, let's move on to the data management lifecycle.

Data Management Lifecycle

For enterprise modernisation and transformation initiatives, we need to consider Big Data as a critical player in the ecosystem. Therefore, digital leaders need to understand the life cycle of Big Data for modernisation and transformation programs. Our roles and responsibilities may differ in different stages in the lifecycle; however, we need to be on top of the life cycle management, especially from the governance perspective, end to end. A typical Big Data solution, similar to traditional data lifecycle, includes several distinct phases in the overall data lifecycle management.

Digital leaders are engaged in all phases of the lifecycle, providing different input for each stage. These phases may have different names in different data solution teams. Digital leaders create a standard naming convention for the phases to bring everyone on the same page. Let's keep in mind that there is no rigorous universal systematic approach to the Big Data lifecycle as the discipline is still evolving. Names and approaches are continually changing based on ongoing experimentations.

At a high level, the data management lifecycle can include foundations, acquisitions, preparation, input, processing, output, interpretation, analytics, consumptions, retention, backup, recovery, archival, and destruction.

As digital leaders, we get involved in all these stages; hence, a broad knowledge of these phases can be beneficial to gain data intelligence. Let's briefly touch on the phases.

Foundation phase includes understanding and validating data requirements, solution scope, roles and responsibilities of stakeholders, data infrastructure preparation, technical and non-technical considerations, and understanding data rules in an organisation.

This phase requires a detailed plan facilitated ideally by a project manager with substantial input from the Big Data solution architects. A PDR (project definition report) must cover the non-technical matters such as project funding, commercials, and other issues. Enterprise Architects govern this phase.

Data Acquisition phase refers to collecting data. We can obtain data from various sources. These sources can be internal and external to the organisation. Data sources can be structured forms such as transferred from a data warehouse, transaction systems, or semi-structured forms such as Web or system logs, or unstructured such as media files consist of videos, audios or pictures.

Data governance, security, privacy, and quality controls start with the data collection phase. The lead data architects document the data collection strategy, requirements, architectural decisions, use cases, and technical specifications in this phase. Digital leaders may need to review and approve the requirements and architectural decisions. Data and platform specialists review and approve the specifications.

In the data preparation phase, we clean the collected raw data. We check the data rigorously for any inconsistencies, errors, and duplicates. We consistently remove any redundant, duplicated, incomplete and incorrect data sets and entries. This activity results in having a clean data set. Preparation of data is usually a specialist level task; however, digital leaders may need to govern this phase. They can delegate the details activities to the data solution architects and specialists.

Data input refers to sending data to planned target data repositories or systems. For example, we send the clean data to determined destinations such as CRM systems, data lakes, or data warehouse. In this phase, we transform the raw data into a useable format. Usually, an Enterprise Architect governs this phase; however, digital leaders may get involved in architecture board activities.

Data Processing starts with processing the raw form of data. Then, we convert data into a readable format giving it the form and context. After this activity, we can interpret data by the selected data analytics tools. We can use generic or proprietary Big Data processing tools based on the data practices in our organisation.

Some standard tools that we may consider are Hadoop MapReduce, Impala, Hive, Pig, and Spark SQL. The most common real-time data processing tool is HBase, and near real-time data processing tools is Spark Streaming. Data processing also includes activities such as data annotation, integration, aggregation, and representation.

In this phase, data may change its format based on requirements. We can use processed data in various data outputs such as in data lakes, for enterprise networks, and connected devices. We can further analyse data using advanced processing techniques and tools such as Spark MLib, Spark GraphX, and machine learning.

Data processing require various team members with different skills sets. While the lead solution architect leads the phase, data specialists, engineers and data scientists perform most of the activities. Enterprise Architects govern this phase from approach, process, technology and tool perspective. Digital leaders may get involved in governance activities.

Data output is a phase where the data is in a format ready for consumption by the business users. We can transform data into useable formats such as plain text, graphs, processed images or video files. This phase announces the data ready for use and sends the data to the next stage for storing. This phase in some organisation is also called data ingestion aiming to export data for immediate use or future use and keep it in a database format. Ingestion process can be a real-time or batch format. We must familiarise with standard Big Data ingestion tools such as Sqoop, Flume, and Spark streaming.

Once we complete the data output phase, we store data in allocated storage units as pointed out by the data platform designs. Once data is stored, then it can be easily accessed by the defined user groups. Big Data storage includes underlying technologies such as relational data storage or extended data storage such as HDFS and HBASE.

We can consider the file formats text, binary, or another type of specialised formats such as Sequence, Avro and Parquet in data storage phase. Several architects and specialists participate in this phase. While digital leaders work with the Enterprise Architects to set the standards, Infrastructure Architects build the data platforms with the input from the Data or Information Architects.

Once the data is stored, in traditional models, it ends the process. However, for Big Data, there may be a need for the integration of stored data for various purposes. Some data models may require integration of data lakes with a data warehouse or data marts. There may also be application integration requirements. For example, some integration activities may comprise of integrating data with dashboards, tableau, websites, or data visualisations applications. This activity may overlap with the next phase, which is data analytics.

Integrated data is ready for data analytics, which is the next phase. Data analytics is a significant component of Big Data. This phase is critical because we gain business value from Big Data. There can be a team responsible for data analytics led by a Data Scientist. Data Architect has a limited role in this phase. Data Architects need to ensure we complete this phase using architectural rigour for analytics. Enterprise Architects validate the standards. Digital leaders can provide guidance and requirements clarification of analytics.

Once data analytics takes place, then we turn data into information ready for consumption by the internal or external users, including customers of the organisation. Some critical data may need to be backed up. There are data backup strategies, techniques, methods and tools that the digital leaders may need to provide guidance to identify, document, and obtain approval.

We may need to archive some critical data for regulatory or other business reasons for a defined period. With the input from digital leaders, Enterprise Architects determine, and document data retention strategy approved by the governing body in the data practice department.

There may be regulatory requirements to destruct a particular type of data after a certain amount of times. These may change based on the industries that data belong. Even though there is a chronological order for the life cycle management, for producing Big Data solutions, some phases may slightly overlap; hence, we can perform them in parallel. The life cycle is the only guideline and can be customised based on the structure of the data solution team, data needs and dynamics of the owner organisation departments or the enterprise.

Usually, Data Architects begins with an understanding of the process end to end. We can classify the process under two broad categories. The first one is Data Management, and the second one is Data Analytics.

It can be useful to understand data management activities such as data acquisition, extraction, cleansing, annotation, processing, integration, aggregation, and representation. Data Analytics components at a high level are activities such as modelling, analysis, interpretation, and visualisation.

Platforms

We need to understand the function of data platforms. The first layer of the data platform is the shared operational information zone consists of the data types such as data in motion, data at rest, and data in several other forms. It includes legacy data sources, new data sources, master data hubs, reference data hubs, and content repositories.

The second large layer is processing. This layer includes data ingestion, operational information, landing area, analytics zone, archive, real-time analytics, exploration, integrated warehouse, data mart zones. This layer needs to have a governance model for metadata catalogue including data security and disaster recovery of systems, storage and hosting and other infrastructure components such as Cloud.

The third layer is the analytics platform. It consists of real-time analytics, planning, forecasting, decision making, predictive analytics, data discovery, visualisations, dashboard, and other analytics features.

The fourth layer consists of outputs such as business processes, decision-making schemes, and point of interactions. We need to provide access with established controls both for the data platform professionals such as Data Scientists, Data Architects, analytics experts, and business users. We need to engage a Security Architect or Specialist to analyse the requirements and take appropriate measures.

Level of the schema for the data platform is a crucial architectural consideration. We can classify the level of schema under three categories, such as no schema, partially structured schema, and full structured schema. Control of schema is an enterprise concern; therefore, Enterprise Architects need to take control of this function with input from digital transformation leaders.

To understand the type of schema, we can use examples. Some examples of no schema are video, audio and picture files; social media feed, partial schema such as email, instant messaging logs, system logs, call centre logs; and high schema can be structured sensor data and relational transaction data.

The data processing levels require architectural considerations. The processing levels could be raw data, validated data, transformed data and calculated data. Another structural classification of data in this platform is related the business relevance. We can categorise the business relevance of data as external data, personal data, departmental data and enterprise data.

Business Vocabulary

Another essential concept is business vocabulary. We need to define business vocabulary as a shared understanding of Big Data related to business analytics. Business vocabulary provides consistent terms to be used by the whole organisation. Business departments own business vocabulary.

Enterprise Architects ensure that this is in place and adequately governed.

Usually, business users maintain this vocabulary. This vocabulary describes the business content supported by the data models. More importantly, from an architectural perspective, this vocabulary can be a crucial input to the metadata catalogue; hence, it can be an enterprise concern.

Data Governance

We must govern data. Data governance is a critical factor for enterprise digital transformation. The Big Data governance system needs to consider essential factors such as security, privacy, trust, operability, conformance, agility, innovation and transformation of data. It is also vital that at a fundamental level, a data governance infrastructure to be established and evolve for adoption at the enterprise level.

Governance may take consideration for different stakeholders in the ecosystem. For example, Data Architects are responsible for developing the governance of Big Data models; Data Scientist is accountable for an analytics perspective. Business stakeholders are responsible for the governance of business models for producing business results for the data ecosystem in concern.

Big Data governance is a broad area and covers components, scope, requirements handling, strategy, architecture, design, development, analysis, tests, processing, components, relationships, input, output, business goals, insights, and all other aspects of data management and analytics.

As digital leaders, we must closely work with Enterprise Architects to maintain governance, especially for digital transformation programs. Enterprise Architects are responsible for end to end governance of Big Data architecture and the associated solutions. They may delegate some governance tasks with Big Data lead and solution architects as required.

Analytics

Big Data Analytics is a comprehensive business-driven discipline. At a high level, it aims to make quick business decisions, reduce the cost for a product or service, and test new market to create new products and services. We use Big Data analytics in all industries. The most commonly used industries are health care, life sciences, manufacturing, government, and retail.

We need methods and tools to perform Big Data Analytics. There are methods and many tools available on the market. As Big Data Analytics is relatively a new discipline, both methods and tools are still evolving. Most of the methods are proprietary; however, some are available via open-source programs. Some popular tools frequently mentioned in the Big Data Analytics publications are Aqua Data Studio, Azure HDinsight, IBM SPSS Modeler, Skytree, Talend, Splice Machine, Plotly, Lumify, Elasticsearch.

Open-source has progressed well in this area and produced multiple powerful tools. Some commonly used open-source analytics tools are Apache Hadoop, Apache Spark, Apache Storm, Apache Cassandra, Apache SAMOA, Neo4j, and MongoDB. We cover the overview of these tools in the technology and tools section of this chapter.

Big Data analytics is a broad and growing area. We need to understand the various methods and techniques used for Big Data Analytics. Most commonly used methods and techniques for Big Data Analytics are natural language processing, two-sample hypothesis testing, machine learning, data mining, association pattern mining, behavioural analytics, predictive analytics, descriptive analytics, prescriptive analytics, diagnostic analytics.

In transforming environments, we deal with predictive analytics in a considerable amount; hence, we need to understand the importance of this technique. Considering current and historical data, predictive analytics cover techniques that predict future outcomes. Predictive analytics look for patterns and capture relationships in data. For example, we can use linear regression techniques in machine learning and neural network to achieve the interdependencies of variables in captured data for predictive analytics. We can use it in many disciplines and various business purposes. Predicting customer purchase goals by analysing their shopping behaviour is an everyday use case for Big Data solutions.

Prescriptive analytics is also essential for digital initiatives. Prescriptive analytics aims to find the best action for a given situation. This type of analysis looks for ways to determine the best outcome among various choices. Prescriptive analytics can be instrumental in mitigating risks, improve the accuracy of predictions, and take benefits of opportunities. This analytics type helps us analyse the interactions and potential decisions and provides the best solution.

There are times we may need to use diagnostic analytics in transformation goals. Diagnostic analytics uses multiple techniques such as discovery, mining, correlations, comparing, and contrasting. Diagnostic analytics ask the question of why something has happened by examining the data and propose an answer to this fundamental question. It can be useful to find the root cause of situations.

For enterprise modernisation and transformation initiatives, we need to keep in mind that emerging data platforms can empower Big Data process and analytics. We touch on some key concepts and the relationships among them in the next section.

Data Lakes

Big Data transformation solutions require the use of the data lake model. Data lakes are fundamental and useful aspects of Big Data lifecycle management. We can define data lakes in the simplest terms as the dynamically clean and instantly useable data sources made available for specific purposes. The need for data lake comes from users to take advantage of clean data based on self-service approach without needing technical data professionals. Use of data lakes can be a critical business proposition for enterprise modernisation and transformation programs.

A data lake can be a single store of transformed enterprise data in the native format. They are usually well reported, visualised and analysed using advanced analytics. A data lake can include structured, semi-structured and unstructured data such as images, videos or sounds.

Data lakes are dynamic stores and can be fed iteratively as further clean data are discovered and transformed from multiple sources in the enterprise. For example, a data lake can store relational data from enterprise applications and non-relational data from IoT devices, social media, and mobile apps.

There are multiple use cases for data lakes. The most common ones are when real-time data analysis required for the data sources coming from various sources. Another use case can be related to the goals of having a complete view of customer data again coming from multiple sources. Auditing requirements and centralisation of data can also be use cases for data lakes. These use cases are relevant and can be significant for enterprise modernisation goals.

The business value of data lakes come from being able to perform advanced analytics very quickly for data coming from various real-time sources such as clickstreams, social media, system logs. Use of data lakes helps the business stakeholders to identify opportunities rapidly, make informed decisions, and act on their decision expeditiously for speed to the market.

Data lakes can be implemented using various tools, techniques, and services. There are commercially available services as well as open-source services to establish data lakes. For example, commercial products such as Azure Data Lake, Amazon S3 and open source product Apache Hadoop file system are some data lake implementation enablers to consider for our solutions. There are many more tools and method to design, implement and execute data lake solutions.

Based on feedback obtained from many successful implementations of data lakes, it appears that an excellent choice of platform for data lakes is Hadoop. Hadoop, as an open-source system, is highly scalable, modular, technology agnostic, open-source, cost-effective and presents no schema limitations. I observed that many digital leaders I worked with and met in other organisations embraced Hadoop due to its effectiveness for transformations.

Designing data lakes require critical consideration of data types. For example, one key consideration is that if the purpose of data is unknown, it is better to keep data in raw format so that it can be used by data professionals in the future when it is needed. Digital leaders can guide these decisions at the enterprise level as far as transformations concerned.

One of the critical challenges of data lakes is security as the data comes to the lake in real-time from multiple uncontrolled sources. To address this challenge, a well-governing security architecture with access controls and semantic consistency need to be in place for the enterprise data lake. Data lake design is a specialist level activity usually conducted by an experienced storage architect or specialist. Digital leaders may provide input to set the standards and maintain the governance for the lifecycle of data lake initiatives.

In addition to data lakes, we also need to understand the data puddles and ponds. Data puddle is a tiny purpose-build data platform usually used by a specific single team mission in an organisation conducted by a marketing group or data scientist. They are also a right candidate for data-intensive ETL (Extract, Transform, Load) offloading engagements for a single team. Unlike data lakes, they are not data-driven processing allowing informed decisions at enterprise levels.

Related to data puddles, another term used for a group of data puddles is data ponds. We can design data ponds for a small amount of data management purposes. One way of explaining a data pond is to resemble it to a data warehouse designed for Big Data processing. Digital leaders can provide input for choosing the right data deployment model with the help of Enterprise, Data and Information Architects.

One more essential term related to data lakes that we need to understand is 'data swamp'. This term refers to an unmanaged data lake that may not be accessible by the intended consumers or may not provide desired business value. From lessons learned in the field, many unsuccessful implementations of data lakes, unfortunately, turned into data swamps.

Let's keep in mind that data swamps are undesirable situations in an enterprise. Thus, as digital leaders, we need to consider these types of hard-learned lessons for data management strategy of the enterprise modernisation and transformation plans.

Essential Considerations for Data Solutions

As digital leaders, we leverage architectural skills, relevant technology, and tools to create custom solutions for transformations. The custom solutions can be products or services depending on the goals and the scope of the transformation programs.

Big Data solutions are distinct and require additional expertise. In addition to considering several architectural points, these solutions also require domain knowledge of data and information architecture. At the highest level, we need to identify optimal approaches to collecting, storing, processing, analysing, and presenting Big Data. However, practical solutions are architected by Big Data or Information Architects with our guiding input.

Big Data solutions require heterogeneous technology and tools to fit the purpose. It is essential to realise that there is no single technology or tool which can provide all-purpose for developing Big Data solutions.

Besides, due to their dependencies and relationships to many components, attributes, and factors, Big Data solutions cannot be developed in isolation or silos. Digital leaders need to consider the entire ecosystem and break the silos in thinking and critical architectural factors that may affect the whole enterprise.

For Big Data solutions, we must focus on highly-scalable platforms, processes, technology, and tools. Due to its nature, scalability is a fundamental requirement for Big Data solutions. Compromising scalability, even in a small amount, can cause undesirable solutions, troubled projects, and failed service levels. Scalability is a critical factor for enterprise modernisation and transformation initiatives.

Modularity is another essential consideration for Big Data solutions for enterprise modernisation goals. For modularity, we need to ensure the modules fits into the big picture. For example, the same data should be able to be used by different projects and technologies rather than creating unnecessary data access silos.

Big Data solutions for digital transformation requires thinking out of the box and innovative ways of doing things. We need to understand the latest technologies and practices for Big Data solutions. For example, there is a trend in the industry for trying new methods of data analysis without binding to traditional EDW resources and ETL processes.

In terms of tools and technologies, we can consider mixing open source and commercial systems based on their applicability and meeting our requirements. For example, OLTP can be designed using commercially available relational databases for structured and open-source Casandra Database supporting semi-structured databases.

Data sources in the enterprise keep changing, and new sources are being available. In addition to legacy data sources, we need to consider new data sources in Big Data modernisation solutions. We need to determine the type of data sources required in our solutions.

From solution readiness and quality management perspectives, it is vital to determine the timelines of data ingestion in the enterprise. Data ingestion, as a critical aspect of Big Data in the modernisation context, is the process of importing, transferring, loading processing and storing data for use. It can be synchronous, or an asynchronous batched, or rea-time basis. We need to articulate these options with compelling reasons and obtain validating input and approvals from subject matter experts and the solution governance body.

It is vital to choose the type of processing to perform whether real-time or batch processing. Our data processing may involve descriptive, predictive, prescriptive, diagnostic, an ad-hoc. We also need to consider the latency expectation of processing. These factors can plan an important role in enterprise modernisation initiatives.

We need to determine how to access the data, for example, by random or sequential order. Besides, we need to consider data access patterns. Data access patterns are necessary to optimise data access requirements. There are many patterns available in data application integration and interface publications. For example, some common patterns are accelerating database resource initialisation, eliminating data access bottlenecks, and hiding obscure database semantics from data users.

Database optimisation is an essential practice at the enterprise level. These techniques aim to improve the quality and speed for data access, read and write activities. Some of the critical considerations are using appropriate indexes, removing unnecessary indexes and minimising data transfers from client to server.

So far, we provided a very high-level view of data considerations at the enterprise level. These are the only tip of the iceberg in developing Big Data solutions for digital transformation. Digital leaders don't go into the details of Big Data architecture as it is a domain level expertise rather than enterprise-level concern. Once we start the process and delve into requirements, we can come across many more considerations based on our industry, project goals and many other factors which some of them can be beyond our controls and may require domain expertise.

Therefore, it is essential to follow an established method, collaborative solution team, proven processes, leading technologies and well-supported tools to produce successful Big Data solutions for digital transformations. Digital leaders can guide the team with these critical foundational data practices. Now let's touch on the magical open source for our digital transformations.

Open Source

I want to highlight the importance of using open-source tools for digital transformations, especially in the data platforms. Use of open source tools can be very beneficial for enterprise modernisation and transformation programs. I assume you are aware of open source but in case, due to its importance, let's briefly touch on the commonly used and recommended Big Data tools in the open-source space.

Open source is incredibly useful and widespread for information technology hence equally crucial for data analytics in the enterprise. It is a type licensing agreement which allows the developers and users to freely use the software, modify it, develop new ways to improve it and integrate to larger projects. It is a collaborative and innovative approach embraced by many IT organisations and consumer organisations. It is not only ideal for start-up companies and those companies with a tight IT budget but also enterprises struggling to have more flexible architectures for modernisation leading to digital transformations.

There are many open-source tools and technologies for Big Data and Analytics. Being familiar with some essential and commonly used open-source tools can be useful. An awareness of these tools is fundamental for us.

Here's a summary of the famous open-source Big Data and Analytics tools. Let's start with famous Hadoop. Apache Hadoop is a platform for data storage and processing. Hadoop is scalable, fault-tolerant, flexible, cost-effective and open source. It is ideal for handling massive storage pools using the batch approach in distributed computing environments. We can use Hadoop for complex Big Data and Analytics solutions at the enterprise level.

The next is Cassandra. Apache Cassandra is a semi-structured open source database. It is linearly scalable, high speed, and fault-tolerant. The primary use case for Cassandra is a transactional system requiring fast response and massive scalability. Cassandra is also widely used for Big Data and Analytics solutions at the enterprise level.

Apache Kafka is a stream processing software platform. Using Kafka, users can subscribe to commit logs and publish data to any number of systems or real-time applications. Kafka offers a unified, high-throughput, low-latency platform for real-time handling data feeds. Kafka platforms were initially developed by LinkedIn, used for a while, and donated to open source.

Apache Flume offers a simple and flexible architecture. The architecture of Flume is a reliable, distributed software for efficiently collecting, aggregating, and moving large amounts of log data in the Big Data ecosystem. We can use Flume for streaming data flows. Flume is fault-tolerant with many failover and recovery systems. Flume uses an extensible data model that allows for online analytic application.

Apache NiFi is an automation tool designed to automate the flow of data amongst the software components based on flow-based programming model. Currently, Cloudera supports for its commercial and development requirements. It has a portal for the users and uses TLS encryption for security.

Apache Samza is a near-real-time stream processing system. It provides an asynchronous framework for stream processing. Samza allows building stateful applications that process data in real-time from multiple sources. It is well known for offering fault tolerance, stateful processing, and isolation.

Apache Sqoop is a command-line interface application used to transfer data between Apache Hadoop and the relational databases. We can use it for incremental loads of a single table or free form SQL queries. We can use Sqoop with Hive and HBase to populate the tables.

Apache Chukwa is a system for data collection. Chukwa monitors large distributed systems and builds on the MapReduce framework on HDFS (Hadoop Distributed File System). Chukwa is a scalable, flexible and robust system for data collection.

Apache Storm is a stream processing framework. The Storm is based on spouts and bolts to define data sources. It allows batch and distributed processing of streaming data. The Storm also enables real-time data processing.

Apache Spark is a framework that allows cluster computing for distributed environments. We can use Spark for general clustering needs. It provides fault tolerance and data parallelism. Spark's architectural foundation is based on resilient distributed dataset. The Dataframe API is an abstraction on top of the resilient distributed dataset. Spark has different editions, such as Core, SQL, Streaming, and GraphX.

Apache Hive is a data warehouse software. We can build Hive on Hadoop platform. Hive provides data query and supports the analysis of large datasets stored in HDFS. It offers a query language called HiveQL.

Apache HBase is a non-relational distributed database. HBase runs on top of HDFS. HBase provides Google's Bigtable-like capabilities for Hadoop. HBase is a fault-tolerant system.

Another great tool, non-Apache is MongoDB. It is a high performance, fault-tolerant, scalable, cross-platform and NoSQL database. It deals with unstructured data. It is developed by MongoDB Inc is licensed under the SSPL (Server-Side Public License), which is a kind of open-source product.

There are many more rapidly developing open-source software tools which can be used for various functions of data life cycle management in the enterprise. These tools can be handy for enterprise modernisation and transformation programs focusing on Big Data and Analytics solutions. These tools are easily accessible and available based on open source licencing agreements.

Commercial Tools

There are also many commercially available tools and technologies for Big Data and Analytics suitable to deploy across enterprise-wide solutions. These tools and technologies can be sold as products or services. An awareness of these products and services can be beneficial for digital leaders. Some of the most popular Big Data and

Analytics platforms with associated tools are Google BigQuery, Hortonworks Data Platform, HP Bigdata, IBM Big Data, Microsoft Azure, SAP Bigdata Analytics, Teradata Bigdata Analytics, Amazon Web Services. As coverage of these platforms and tools is comprehensive and exhaustive, it is beyond the scope of this book to include them here.

Chapter Summary and Take Away Points

One significant fact is that data, especially Big Data, is ubiquitous in every enterprise.

Big data is different from traditional data. The main differences come from characteristics such as volume, velocity, variety, veracity, value and overall complexity of data sets in a data ecosystem.

At a high level, the data management lifecycle can include foundations, acquisitions, preparation, input, processing, output, interpretation, analytics, consumptions, retention, backup, recovery, archival, and destruction.

Some standard tools that we may consider are Hadoop MapReduce, Impala, Hive, Pig, and Spark SQL.

Once data analytics takes place, then we turn data into information ready for consumption by the internal or external users, including customers of the organisation.

There may be regulatory requirements to destruct a particular type of data after a certain amount of times.

The data processing levels require architectural considerations. The processing levels could be raw data, validated data, transformed data and calculated data. Another structural classification of data in this platform is related the business relevance. We can categorise the business relevance of data as external data, personal data, departmental data and enterprise data.

Business vocabulary describes the business content supported by the data models. More importantly, from an architectural perspective, this vocabulary can be a crucial input to the metadata catalogue; hence, it can be an enterprise concern.

The Big Data governance system needs to consider essential factors such as security, privacy, trust, operability, conformance, agility, innovation and transformation of data. It is also vital that at a fundamental level, a data governance infrastructure to be established and evolve for adoption at the enterprise level.

There are methods and many tools available on the market. As Big Data Analytics is relatively a new discipline, both methods and tools are still evolving.

Data lakes are fundamental and useful aspects of Big Data lifecycle management. We can define data lakes in the simplest terms as the dynamically clean and instantly useable data sources made available for specific purposes.

Big Data solutions require heterogeneous technology and tools to fit the purpose. It is essential to realise that there is no single technology or tool which can provide all-purpose for developing Big Data solutions.

Open source is incredibly useful and widespread for information technology hence equally crucial for data analytics in the enterprise. It is a type licensing agreement which allows the developers and users to freely use the software, modify it, develop new ways to improve it and integrate to larger projects.

Some of the most popular Big Data and Analytics platforms with associated tools are Google BigQuery, Hortonworks Data Platform, HP Bigdata, IBM Big Data, Microsoft Azure, SAP Bigdata Analytics, Teradata Bigdata Analytics, Amazon Web Services.

Chapter 12: Mobile Intelligence

Purpose

We use and work with mobile devices every day. Mobile Intelligence is critical to digital modernisation and transformation. Mobility is so crucial that the whole digital approach revolves around enterprise, product and services mobility.

Mobility

Mobility involves people, process, technology and tools at a massive scale. Mobility is essential for people in the enterprise. The demand for mobility is rapidly increasing. The process for mobility is also challenged to meet the demands of consumers. Technology and tools are proliferating. Mobile devices, mobile phones, mobile computers, tablets, wireless networks are a few to mention.

Lifecycle

Lifecycle management for mobile devices is an essential architectural consideration in enterprise modernisation and transformation initiatives. Managing mobile devices can be daunting from many angles. The life cycle for mobile devices can be much shorter than traditional computing and telecommunication devices.

Dealing with Quantity

Another architectural challenge related to mobile devices is dealing with quantity. In the past, there were only office phones and people used to share them. Nowadays, workers have multiple mobile phones. Having multiple mobile devices per person may equate to thousands of mobile devices to consider at the enterprise level.

In addition to quantity, the user in the enterprise may change the mobile devices frequently. These frequent changes require consideration of applications and software updates for these devices.

Enterprise modernisation and transformation strategies must consider the challenges associated with these mobile devices. Digital leaders need to create dynamic and flexible governance to address the concerns related to the use and lifecycle management of these devices.

Mobile Security Implications

The security implications of mobile devices are massive challenges. They create many security vulnerabilities for enterprises. Software updates can be persistent and very frequent. Frequent updates and patching can create a massive workload for the IT support departments.

Use of these mobile devices increases information consumption in the enterprise dramatically. Security control of the data can be daunting too. These security implications cross the data and application domains; hence, a collaborative effort among the Security, Data and Application Architects are required. Digital leaders must coordinate this collaboration across other technical, architectural and business domains in the enterprise.

These critical challenges created by mobile devices are real and evident in the enterprise. Therefore, enterprise modernisation initiative must consider these challenges and find practical and innovative ways to address them.

Mobile Business Intelligence

Mobile business intelligence, also known as Mobile BI is an essential requirement for enterprises to stay competitive, open new markets, and create new revenue streams. Mobile BI includes both real-time and historical information for analysing mobile devices such as phones and tablets. The primary purpose of Mobile BI is to provide insights, based on past and current information, for business decision making.

Mobile BI is necessary for the overall support of mobile devices in the enterprise ecosystem. This intelligence, providing a broad perspective on the business data, sales figures, consumption figures and performance statistics, can be valuable for enterprise modernisation. By using the analytics on mobile progress in an enterprise can be very useful to develop a new business model and improve the current models.

Product and service providers widely use Mobile BI. Some established and popular Mobile BI environments are publicly accessible services such as Appstore by Apple, Google Play Store, and Samsung Galaxy Store. Enterprise modernisation programs can model these well-functioning services to create and improve their current Mobile BI strategy, service models, and offerings.

Unified Endpoint Management

A unified endpoint management (UEM) practice is essential for enterprise modernisation and transformation initiatives. UEM includes relevant software tools and centralised management interfaces for consumers.

This centralisation is necessary to improve the security capabilities and also allow a collaborative content sharing for the consumers and other stakeholders. We need to integrate unified endpoint management to our enterprise modernisation program structure.

Conclusive Remarks for Mobility

Mobility is an inevitable part of our lives at home and in the workplace. Fortunately, or unfortunately, it created a bridge between homes and workplaces. In some ways, employers can easily access their employees; however, the privacy of employees are affected by this easy accessibility.

The reality is that we cannot do business without the use of mobile devices any more. Mobility is an essential part of the enterprise. It touches every aspect of the enterprise. We cannot have a digital workplace without proper mobility architecture in place.

We cannot have a modern enterprise without including the mobility to the equation. Due to these compelling reasons, we must approach mobility from strategic and architectural perspectives to properly integrate it into the culture and ecosystem of the modernising and transformation enterprise.

Chapter Summary and Take Away Points

Managing mobile devices can be daunting from many angles. The life cycle for mobile devices can be much shorter than traditional computing and telecommunication devices.

Nowadays, workers have multiple mobile phones. Having multiple mobile devices per person may equate to thousands of mobile devices to consider at the enterprise level.

The security implications of mobile devices are massive challenges. They create many security vulnerabilities for enterprises.

Mobile business intelligence, also known as Mobile BI is an essential requirement for enterprises to stay competitive, open new markets, and create new revenue streams.

The reality is that we cannot do business without the use of mobile devices any more. Mobility is an essential part of the enterprise. It touches every aspect of the enterprise. We cannot have a digital workplace without proper mobility architecture in place.

Chapter 13: Digital Team Intelligence

Purpose

A digital ecosystem can be consisting of many interrelated teams with a wide variety of professionals covering various facets of enterprise modernisation and digital transformations. We can see many roles and responsibilities in these programs.

These roles and responsibilities need to be known and understood clearly. Therefore, we named this chapter digital team intelligence.

Understanding digital team structures and dynamics require a considerable amount of intelligence. Let's discuss the significant factors in subsequent sections.

Digital Talent

Talent is essential in enterprise modernisation and transformation initiatives. Therefore, as digital leaders, we need to understand the value and importance of talent for our programs. Without calibre talent, our digital programs cannot progress and transform productively.

To this end, we need to be very cautious to nurture and keep talent in our teams. We need to make every effort to retain valuable talent in our teams. We cannot emphasise enough that talent is a crucial enabler of core products and services of modernising enterprises. Without talent, an organisation cannot be competitive in its modernisation goals. There is a constant talent hunting in the industry to secure these scarce resources.

We need to perform talent management and facilitation roles. We can encourage the less junior team members to perform better and turn them into talented team players.

We can also pick up poor performance in our team and help remove poorly performing employees and replace them with talented team members who can genuinely contribute to the modernisation and transformation vision. Our success depends on high-performance teams.

Team Performance

Enterprise modernisation and transformation initiatives require team members who can perform and produce at the highest possible level. These team members must perform optimally at all times to meet the challenges of these programs. Their skills and capabilities must be tested and validated to suit the type of work they are performing.

Building high-performance teams are critical for the success of these programs. We need to create proactive and engaged local technical teams and community of practices as give back activities. These high-quality teams and collaborative community of practices can generate innovative, high-quality solutions in agility. They are ideal contributors to modernisation, digital transformation, and fusion goals.

As these teams are involved in complex matters, people may have blind spots to understand the sophisticated dynamics. Blind spots can be hazardous in digital teams. The owner of the blind spot cannot see his or her blind spot unless using specific tools or assistance from someone else who is more experienced. Habits and habitual thinking patterns are common causes of blind spots. Focusing on details without seeing the big picture can also cause cloudy thinking and ultimately dangerous blind spots.

However, as astute digital leaders, we need to look for big pictures from multiple angles and deep dive when needed hence can quickly identify blind spots and weaknesses experienced by our team members.

We need to articulate situations with constructive feedback, lots of clarifying examples, metaphors, and similes. This influential articulation focus can help people to see their blind spots, understand their weaknesses, and turn them into strengths. Related to blind spots, identifying hidden agendas and hidden costs are critical for enterprise modernisation initiatives.

Taking necessary performance measures are essential for enterprise modernisation and transformation programs. We need to focus on both qualitative and quantitative measures for team success. We can manage across complex matrix structures in our organisations.

As metric oriented digital professionals, we need to use KPIs (Key Performance Indicators). We can use a team dashboard to see the trends and qualify and quantify progress in visual formats for the team members and the business stakeholders.

We need to encourage other team members to create their dashboard and shared dashboard for the team. Our teams must turn the enterprise to a data-driven organisation to measure the progress of modernisation goals structurally and methodically. One of the key measures is customer orientation and support mechanisms.

We ensure a customer-centric outlook is provided, focusing on continually improving client experience with measurable results. We are expected to be the 'thought leaders. Thought leadership is a critical need and demand in modernisation environments, for changing cultures, and transforming ecosystems.

Tangible outcomes are essential for the success of enterprise modernisation and transformation programs. These programs require tangible outcomes iteratively rather than monolithic. For example, some tangible outcomes can be a virtualisation of platforms, creating containers, creating reusable shared resources, reviewed products, and agreed services.

We need to pay special attention to providing measurable outcomes with the support of our team members. The modernising environment presents a constant and rapid change and any change matters in the transforming ecosystem. These small and rapid changes lead to more significant measurable outcomes at later stages of the modernisation; for example, the systems may need to be fully automated, loosely coupled, service-oriented, software-defined, self-learning, self-managing, and self-healing are a few to mention in this context.

Digital Professionals

As digital leaders, we work with many professionals involved in digital initiatives in our organisations. For example, we closely work with architects, designers, and technical specialists. At the highest level, applying a rigorous enterprise architecture approach is a critical aspect of modernisation and transformation initiatives.

Let's beware that if the enterprise architecture process goes wrong in an initiative, everything else goes wrong. All other architecture types, such as solution architecture, system architecture, integration architecture, and other architecture domains, are all dependent on the quality of enterprise architecture. Apart from architecture, the subsequent activities in the modernisation life cycle are also adversely affected.

After a validated, business-focused, and pragmatic architecture supporting the modernisation and transformation strategy, the design (both high level and detailed level) is the next vital aspect to be considered in the lifecycle.

We participate in various forums such as the Architecture Review Boards and Design Authority forums. These forums are consisting of many architects, designers and technical specialists. For example, a Design Authority maybe consist of multiple architects with diverse expertise in different domains. Usually, Enterprise Architects orchestrate the activities with their broad knowledge and understanding of the strategy, architecture, technical matters, and business. They govern the Design Authority by using their organisational skills coupled with other architectural skills and business understanding. Let's understand the role of Enterprise Architects as we must work with them day to day basis in our transformation programs.

Enterprise Architects

Enterprise Architects have strategic, architectural thinking, and design thinking skills. These esteemed architects need to articulate the current enterprise environment to the sponsoring senior executives, set future enterprise environment goals, and show how to bridge the gap for modernisation goals between these two environments.

At a high level, Enterprise Architects understand the overall digital modernisation and transformation scope, requirements, and use cases of the solutions. Besides, Enterprise Architects perform Viability Assessments which are critical to enterprise modernisation and transformation programs. These architects must regularly assess risks, issues, dependencies and constraints considering strengths, weaknesses, opportunities and threats in their day to day tasks.

Enterprise Architects are responsible and accountable for architectural and technical governance. Technical governance is an essential aspect of modernisation initiatives. The modernisation programs require particular governance model due to their nature. A dynamic and flexible governance model is essential for modernisation initiatives. The traditional stringent and extreme rule-based oppressive governance models can be roadblocks to the progress. Agility principles best suit to the dynamic governance models.

Enterprise Architects usually perform the role of technical governance head in sizeable modernisation programs. They can have formal governance roles. For example, these architects can run the architecture review boards or design authority forums established for complex modernisation programs.

Business Domain Architects

Business Domain Architects usually assigned to a specific business domain in an enterprise and play various roles and responsibilities in digital modernisation and transformation programs.

Domain Architects can architect a component or integrated components in their business units. Even though they are business focussed, they can also have a strong technical background covering various aspects of architecture such as infrastructure, applications, data, security and more.

When we are working for a specific business unit problem, these domain architects can be instrumental in providing required guidance to our initiatives.

Infrastructure Architects

Infrastructure Architects are responsible for the underlying infrastructure such as network, servers, storage, platforms, physical facilities such as data centres and communications. These architects are responsible for the plumbing of the digital world. As digital leaders, we closely work with these architects as they are astute about the infrastructure components of our digital initiatives.

Application Architects

Application Architects are responsible for applications and middleware across the enterprise. Enterprises can have many standalone and integrated applications spanning across multiple servers, domains and geographic locations.

Application Architects understand the functionality, operability, supportability, integration, and migration of applications.

As digital leaders, we closely work with Application Architects. They are critical resources for digital modernisation and transformation programs.

Specialist Architects

Even though architects cover breadth, some architects specialise in particular areas in the enterprise due to the extensive scope of the domains. The most common specialty areas are Security Architect, Data Architect, Information Architect, Network Architect, Mobility Architect, Workplace Architect. Some of these types of architects can also serve as a technical specialist which we cover in the next section.

Technical Specialists

As digital leaders, we work closely with technical specialists who have distinct technology expertise covering a broad spectrum of technologies in all technical domains. These specialists are technically eminent professionals in their chosen field. In some organisations, they are called distinguished specialists.

Technical eminence or distinguished refers to outstanding technical expertise recognised internally and externally to the organisation of a technical leader who is influential and high impact to both technical and business communities.

Some technical specialists have strong industry skills, demonstrate thought leadership, and possess multiple domain expertise. These specialists are highly regarded and sought after for their views and contributions to modernisation and transformation initiatives. Leading the enterprise for modernisation requires distinguishing factors in multiple technology domains with in-depth understanding to some extent. These groups of people are ideal talents for digital transformation programs.

Business Analysts

Business Analysts are critical resources to translate business requirements to technical requirements working with business stakeholders, architects, and technical specialists.

Exceptional communication skills are essential for Business Analysts dealing with modernisation and transformation initiatives. Their communication skills are well respected and sought after by their peers, managers, and customers.

Business Analysts are expected to communicate at all levels with confidence and ease. They must articulate the most complex situations and technical matters to all stakeholders in a language that those people can understand. Business Analysts must customise their messages based on audience profile.

Digital Mentors and Coaches

Mentoring and coaching is a cultural shift and the essential requirement of modernising environments. There must be a constant nurturing and knowledge transfer from top to bottom. To this end, as digital leaders, we must be mentors for our team members, other team members, people from partnering organisations, students from universities, and even external people in other organisations.

We need to generously share our knowledge and transfer them to anyone who needs such knowledge to utilise in modernisations and transformation engagements.

We also need to be good at coaching our peers, subordinates, and cross-team members by being a soundboard to them. Junior team members can be easily overwhelmed by the rapid pace and changes of modernisation programs.

We can be excellent listeners and even contribute to the wellbeing of our team members providing coaching sessions for stressful colleagues resulting in therapeutic outcomes.

Agile and Change Champions

Change is critical for enterprise modernisation and transformation. Everything changes continuously and rapidly. Change leadership is a vital function for modernisation. Dealing with rapid change is non-trivial, and indeed require delicate skills, experience, and insights.

As digital leaders, we must be catalysts for ongoing change and serve as an Agile Champion. With our catalytical contributions, we need to refresh the culture to more agile, collaborative, inventive, and innovative landscapes in the enterprise.

As change and agile champion, we can create innovative sets of practices in the ecosystem. Our attributes, such as being responsive, sharing and learning mutually, and having fun with joy in a pleasant team environment, can have a tremendous impact on improving the culture for positive change.

Team Learning

Learning is a never-ending process in transformational environments leading towards modernisation of legacy enterprise. Due to changing technologies, process and tools, as digital leaders, we need to learn rapidly and efficiently.

We can have a wide variety of learning styles. Based on situations and conditions, we need to learn formally and informally based on circumstances. We need to turn every possible interaction to a potential learning opportunity.

We must create learning opportunities only for ourselves but also for team members. We also need to teach other people actively and on-demand. By teaching our team members, we can even learn more and better. This new way of learning is critical to meet the demands of enterprise modernisation and transformation goals.

Chapter Summary and Take Away Points

Talent is essential in enterprise modernisation and transformation initiatives. We need to understand the value and importance of talent for our programs. Without calibre talent, our digital programs cannot progress and transform productively.

Building high-performance teams are critical for the success of these programs. We need to create proactive and engaged local technical teams and community of practices as give back activities.

We need to focus on both qualitative and quantitative measures for team success. We can manage across complex matrix structures in our organisations.

As metric oriented digital professionals, we need to use KPIs (Key Performance Indicators). We can use a team dashboard to see the trends and qualify and quantify progress in visual formats for the team members and the business stakeholders.

Enterprise Architects have strategic, architectural thinking, and design thinking skills.

Domain Architects can architect a component or integrated components in their business units.

Infrastructure Architects are responsible for the underlying infrastructure such as network, servers, storage, platforms, physical facilities such as data centres and communications.

Application Architects understand the functionality, operability, supportability, integration, and migration of applications.

The most common specialty areas are Security Architect, Data Architect, Information Architect, Network Architect, Mobility Architect, Workplace Architect.

Technical specialists have distinct technology expertise covering a broad spectrum of technologies in all technical domains. These specialists are technically eminent professionals in their chosen field.

Business Analysts are critical resources to translate business requirements to technical requirements working with business stakeholders, architects, and technical specialists.

Mentoring and coaching is a cultural shift and the essential requirement of modernising environments. There must be a constant nurturing and knowledge transfer from top to bottom.

As digital leaders, we must be catalysts for ongoing change and serve as an Agile Champion.

Due to changing technologies, process and tools, as digital leaders, we need to learn rapidly and efficiently.

Chapter 14: Conclusions

Congratulations, we reached the conclusions after covering many facets of digital intelligence. Now, let's take a high-level review of what we learned to reinforce our learning and comprehension. Now let's have a quick recap of the key points we discussed earlier.

We covered that the standard definition of intelligence is the ability to acquire knowledge and skills and apply them as needed. Digital intelligence, at a high level, is the ability to convert or represent the physical world in digital format.

Physical and digital are two different worlds with dissimilar entities. They have their inherent capabilities and limitations. To be digitally intelligent, we need to have in-depth knowledge of the digital process and acquire practical skills relevant to the digital disciplines.

Architectural thinking can be used as a robust framework to gain digital knowledge, unfold the mystery of digital intelligence, and increase our digital intelligence by providing a structured approach.

Vision sets the scene and shows us where we want to be in the future. Even though everyone has a vision, a productive and strategic vision is a leadership capability and requires a substantial amount of intelligence, knowledge, skills, and experience.

Our digital strategy helps us reach our destination using a master plan. The master plan can be a high-level roadmap to take us to the destination we set.

Both users and systems have their requirements. There are different requirements for different kinds of users. Requirements gathering for digital endeavours are an end to end process such as collecting, analysing, clarifying, tracking, validating, and using.

Dealing with use cases require different thinking modes, such as looking at things from the user's perspective. Observing and being an observer at the same time is a critical mental capability.

By understanding the current state, we set future state and develop a roadmap to reach the target goals. Architectural thinking can guide us to think the feasibility of our digital solution roadmap looking at the risks, dependencies and the constraints on the way.

A trade-off is a compromise between two options. When making trade-offs, we need to consider critical factors, such as cost, quality, functionality, usability and many other non-functional items.

We need to make architectural decisions very carefully as each decision can have a severe impact and multiple implications. Some implications can be cost-related, while others can relate to performance, availability, security and scalability.

Setting the context for any solution help us communicate it to relevant stakeholders in an efficient manner. Context adds clarity to understanding the solution.

A model is the proposed structure typically on a smaller scale than its original. Describing abstract representations in concrete details also requires a great deal of mental exercise, including dealing with multiple patterns, which can stimulate our thinking abilities.

Dealing with complexity requires extensive intelligence. The most common technique is simplifying complexity by using a partitioning approach. We can divide, subdivide, segregate, or apportion the systems, objects, or components, or teams to smaller units.

One way of simplifying a system is reducing the number of repetitive constituents. Another technique could be moving an item from a large group of the clustered items but still, keep the relationship to preserve its core identity. After partitioning and simplifying, the following useful method is iterating.

Everything in enterprise transformation generates substantial cost. There are known and hidden costs.

Hidden costs are the more significant part of the proverbial iceberg.

We can contribute to reducing the solution costs by making trade-offs with a methodical and collaborative approach.

We increase the quality of the solutions by applying professional diligence, architectural rigour, delivery agility, smart collaboration across multiple teams, and harvesting re-usable materials.

Beware that there may be tremendous pressure from project managers and procurement staff to generate an upfront Bill of Materials due to demands of the project lifecycle. However, we can point out that without an approved architecture and design, we cannot commence purchasing materials.

There can be extensive infrastructure and maintenance costs associated with large data centres, server farms, mobile devices, storage units, data processing tools, analytics machines, and hosting in multi-Clouds.

Automated SLAs can detect low availability and poor performance. These automated SLAs trigger the rules and force the organisations breaching the agreements pay the contractually agreed penalties.

We need to pay attention to the SLAs from the nascent stages of the digital solution life cycle. The higher the quality of the solutions, the easier it is for SLAs to meet when the solutions are in production and the operational state. The rigour for quality in each phase can positively contribute to deal with SLA risks.

Some of the key considerations to address SLA issues could be autonomous condition monitoring and remote maintenance.

Digital transformations are long journeys moving the enterprises from chaos to coherence. The transformation process includes every aspect of the enterprise. Enterprise digital systems can include business IT processes, business data, business applications, IT infrastructure, and IT service delivery. These domains can even be more complicated with the addition of geographical factors such as adding multiple countries to the equation.

One of the essential workaround solutions for dealing with this complexity is to modernise these primary domains iteratively in parallel.

The strategy document is a critical artefact to bring all parties and stakeholders on the same page. Then the digital solution leaders identify the critical dependencies among these domains based on the short term, midterm and long-term considerations.

A viability assessment must include key risks, constraints, and dependencies. The viability assessment can be the most informative tool a digital solution lead can provide to the sponsoring executives to make informed decisions.

As the digital solution leads, we need to develop criteria to prioritise the requirements based on factors depicted in the strategy and roadmap documents, as well as the financial and business priorities set by the sponsoring executives.

We need to introduce innovation continuously, as a cost reduction enabler, as it can be the dominant player for overall cost management in complex digital environments.

Innovation and invention relate to novelty, improvement, iterations, and ongoing steady progress. Innovative and inventive thinking generates novel ideas, focuses on improving ideas, and strives for making continuous iterative progress.

Enterprise cultures embracing innovative and inventive thinking approaches can naturally renew themselves to survive and thrive in fluctuating conditions, which are typical in modernising and transforming enterprises.

Innovation, inventions, technical excellence, and agility are interrelated. Innovative and inventive thinking ignites technical excellence, and technical excellence can be empowered by agility.

We usually use vertical and linear types of thinking for problem-solving. Applying logic and streamlining thoughts are some techniques in this type of thinking mode. Horizontal thinking covering more breadth rather than depth aims to generate unpredictable ideas by breaking out the rigid thought patterns. Horizontal thinking challenges the assumptions. This type of thinking looks for alternatives and goes beyond the ordinary, creating radical solutions.

Some commonly used techniques for horizontal thinking are randomisations, distortions, reversals, exaggerations, metaphors, analogies, dreaming, theme mining, questioning the norms, and creating contradictions.

One of the practical techniques to generate innovative and inventive ideas is to use mind mapping. We can articulate our thoughts using representative maps on paper or a whiteboard.

People collaborate better in cultures embracing innovative and inventive ideas. They see themselves with the changing conditions in new positions. They do not resist as they know that change can be useful for them.

The best way for to ignite innovation and invention is to be a role model for our followers. We need to encourage the team members to innovate, invent and reward them for their achievements.

In modernising organisations, innovation and invention become habitual. Team members strive for excellence by creating new ideas in their day to day tasks. We not only need to create innovations and inventions at a personal level but also through collaboration with the immediate teams and extended teams.

Design thinking allows the team to be intuitive and logical at the same time. Design thinking enables team members to be more creative to recognise new patterns.

We need to have a growth mindset to ignite innovation and invention in the ecosystem. We must help our team members with a fixed mindset to convert to a growth mindset.

We must be customer-centric and put ourselves in customers' shoes with strong empathy. Using design thinking techniques, we can develop empathy maps. The mindset based on empathy is part of the design thinking practice.

We need to consider market conditions and the needs of clients. These conditions can help us generate new ideas. Listening to our clients carefully and collaborating with them can help us focus on innovative thinking. Many innovations can be co-created with clients.

There can be many visible and invisible roadblocks to innovation; therefore, it is critical to recognise potential roadblocks. The roadblocks can be in various forms and from various angles. One of the main roadblocks is keeping the status quo.

There is always an unknown fear and resistance towards novelties by some people who may have hidden agendas. We must recognise those people who may try to sabotage innovative and inventive thinking in the modernisation programs.

We must find ways to engage resisting people and show the value and benefit of new ideas to these types of people. The business as usual mentality can be a roadblock for new ideas. Cumbersome business processes can be deterrent factors. More importantly, tired employees can hardly have any interest in innovation and inventions as they cannot see the immediate need.

Simplicity touches almost every angle of modernisation solutions, as these solutions can incredibly complex. Simplicity, in sophisticated enterprises, is a paradoxical topic. Paradoxically, to create simplicity, one needs to deal with a lot of complexity, complications and sophisticated matters.

Digitally intelligent leaders are expected to articulate the most complicated and complex matters in a simple format that is understandable by others.

One of the effective ways to this simplification is automating routine tasks and repetitive technology stacks. Automation can help standardise and simplify convoluted and repetitive tasks prone to human errors.

We need to have a mission to simplify the business and technology processes and make them user-centric.

The sophisticated services model in the back office requires substantial amounts of simplification for users to take benefits of using complicated technologies.

Simplicity and clarity are closely related. Especially in the technical services industry, providing a transparent experience to the technical team members can be very beneficial.

Design simplicity has a tremendous impact on the subsequent phases of the modernisation lifecycle, such as service delivery and support. The simpler the design, the more effective the delivery and service support can be.

Mobile designs must focus on simplicity by removing clutter from screens due to the nature of small screen views. These types of designs must focus on only fundamentally essential objects.

Modularity and modular approaches to complex solutions are essential for simplification, modernisation, and digital transformation. One of the approaches for the modernisation goals can be a domain-based walkthrough of simplifying modules of IT infrastructure, applications, architecture, middleware, security, network, and data domains.

Convoluted specifications also require simplification. For many years, time and energy spent on the system and user specification of software and hardware products and services were substantial.

User stories are simple templates, including the functionalities, capabilities, and specifications from users or consumers point of view.

The simplification process for communication enables to facilitate understanding of issues, risks and dependencies effectively.

Refraining from convoluted phrases and instead, use of precise language and explicit statements are essential factors in simplifying communication.

While we can use advanced business terms to senior executives to articulate a point, we need to use deep technical terms to talk with engineers or technical specialists. This awareness, customisation, and flexibility in communication is a crucial characteristic of digital leaders.

The attention span for our generation is relatively low due to many technical disruptions in our lives.

To this end, digital leaders must get the point quickly before losing the attention of people.

While having this rigour, we also need to have a balance for delivering the message in the simplest possible terms and making the processes for governance in the most effective ways.

One way of simplifying data is to clean data, remove duplications and errors. Reducing data sources and volumes when needed are also used to simplify data management processes.

We can achieve data simplicity through the right data analysis, intelligence, powerful tools, and effective management strategies.

Our presentations must be concise and to the point. Dead from PowerPoint is a famous statement depicting inefficiencies of presentations using an excessive number of slides.

Speed to market is one of the most fundamental requirements of businesses nowadays. We can generate revenues only by acting very quickly.

An agile approach allows the team members to test their ideas iteratively. If they fail, they fail quickly and cheaply without costing lots of funds to the initiatives.

Agile methods require multiple roles. The most common ones are the scrum master and the product owner. Accelerated intelligence for digital requires developing quick mental models on how technology users interact with their solution in each iteration.

The notion of perfection equates to failure in fast-paced transformation programs. Taking extended times is not feasible in this digital age any more. Consumers expect product and services much quicker than old times. Our profitability depends on our speed to market.

Use of evolving methods such as DevOps is also prime considerations for enabling modernisation leading to substantial digital transformations. DevOps brings the software development and infrastructure support operations teams together in an integrated way.

Applying automation and standardisation to our digital transformation objectives, we can reduce the number of resources required to maintain manual and tedious tasks.

Automation and standardisation can address human errors and resolve potential errors quickly. Enterprises embracing agile cultures do not resist automation and standardisation; in fact, they leverage the capabilities for modernisation and transformation goals.

Silos are proven to slow the whole enterprise modernisation and transformation lifecycle. By leveraging the agile principles, we can pay special attention to collaboration, co-locations, and face to face teamwork rather than having silos and hierarchies in our organisations.

We continuously must focus on the priority items and deal with the backlog items based on priority orders.

One of the critical aspects of agile intelligence is the creation of a minimum viable product using agile principles. Managing every user story, clearing a backlog item on a timely basis, and running a sprint is all about constant change.

Agile methods enable the principles of the fail fast, fail early, fail cheaply. These principles are fundamental success factors for modernisation and digital transformation goals.

Agile is a cost-focused and revenue-generating approach. As agile digital leaders, we are capable of turning costs to investment.

In its true meaning, collaboration refers to a team of people working together for mutual goals to achieve successful and synergetic outcomes.

The term fusion refers to joining different things with different attributes or functions together to create a single new entity or form. The notion of fusion relates to concepts such as integration, blending, merging, amalgamation, synergy, and bonding.

Fusion is the most advanced and effective type of collaboration especially required for complex and complicated modernisation initiatives with unique goals and market focus. Creating fusion-based collaboration can be very challenging.

Effective communication is a critical enabler of fusion goals. Depending on the medium, both verbal and written communication types are essential for fusion to happen.

The power of connected people from diverse backgrounds for the same goal generates new ideas and insights. Some of these ideas and insights may touch people from different angles and further motivate them even to take more responsibilities in this transforming ecosystem.

This magical aspect of fusion and collaboration leading to innovation is an ideal situation for transforming the enterprise.

As digital leaders, we influence our collaborators by demonstrating responsibility, accountability, and credibility. We can earn the trust of our collaborators with credibility and integrity. Consistency and predictability for our behaviour are critical factors for credibility.

We can establish diversity with trust. When people start showing their true self, a diverse culture starts flourishing. Diversity is an enhancer of collaboration and fusion.

The key technology enablers of enterprise modernisation and transformation goals are Cloud Computing, Mobile technologies, IoT, Big Data, and Data Analytics.

The most significant attribute of Cloud is that the cloud service model can expand or reduce computer resources based on service requirements. Flexible workload movement is another crucial attribute of Cloud service model. There may be times an organisation requires to run their workloads in a different time zone, and the workloads can easily be moved to a data centre in another country.

In the market, it is noticeable that IoT technologies are emerging and IoT solutions are growing exponentially. Consumers and service providers have an incredible interest and focus on IoT powered by the internet.

Big Data and Analytics are vital technologies and processes that we need to understand. The Big Data process refers to capturing a substantial amount of data from multiple sources, storing analysing, searching, transferring, sharing, updating, visualising and governing huge volumes data such as petabytes or even exabytes.

Big Data analytics is a broad and growing area. We can better understand Big data analytics looking at its inherent characteristics. They are connection, conversion, cognition, configuration, content, customisation, cloud, cyber, and community.

Machine learning is a trending discipline. It is widely adopted. Machine learning refers to computer systems to learn and improve based on their learning from the analysis of large volumes of data sets without programming.

Text analytics include machine learning, computational linguistics, and traditional statistical analysis. Text analytics focus on converting massive volumes of a machine or human-generated text into meaningful structures to create business insights and support decision-making.

NLP is commonly used in various commercial products such as Siri by Apple, Watson by IBM, and Alexa by Amazon products.

Cybersecurity is a vast security domain covering every aspect of security management, such as identity and access management, authentication, authorisation, encryption, and many more areas.

Since the network and associated communication technologies are the fundamental enablers of enterprise modernisation goals, understanding functions of network and network implications such as security, latency, bandwidth, are also important topics.

Mobility is associated with several architectural and business considerations such as network access, compliance, data management, workplace demographics, end-user accountability and BYOD concepts.

IT service management includes processes such as change, problem, incident, service level, capacity, availability, business continuity, and security management. Knowledge of ITIL can be handy in communicating our service management needs to broader stakeholders in the enterprise.

One significant fact is that data, especially Big Data, is ubiquitous in every enterprise. Big data is different from traditional data. The main differences come from characteristics such as volume, velocity, variety, veracity, value and overall complexity of data sets in a data ecosystem.

At a high level, the data management lifecycle can include foundations, acquisitions, preparation, input, processing, output, interpretation, analytics, consumptions, retention, backup, recovery, archival, and destruction. Some standard tools that we may consider are Hadoop MapReduce, Impala, Hive, Pig, and Spark SQL.

Once data analytics takes place, then we turn data into information ready for consumption by the internal or external users, including customers of the organisation. There may be regulatory requirements to destruct a particular type of data after a certain amount of times.

The data processing levels require architectural considerations. The processing levels could be raw data, validated data, transformed data and calculated data. Another structural classification of data in this platform is related the business relevance. We can categorise the business relevance of data as external data, personal data, departmental data and enterprise data.

Business vocabulary describes the business content supported by the data models. More importantly, from an architectural perspective, this vocabulary can be a crucial input to the metadata catalogue; hence, it can be an enterprise concern.

The Big Data governance system needs to consider essential factors such as security, privacy, trust, operability, conformance, agility, innovation and transformation of data. It is also vital that at a fundamental level, a data governance infrastructure to be established and evolve for adoption at the enterprise level.

There are methods and many tools available on the market. As Big Data Analytics is relatively a new discipline, both methods and tools are still evolving.

Data lakes are fundamental and useful aspects of Big Data lifecycle management. We can define data lakes in the simplest terms as the dynamically clean and instantly useable data sources made available for specific purposes.

Big Data solutions require heterogeneous technology and tools to fit the purpose. It is essential to realise that there is no single technology or tool which can provide all-purpose for developing Big Data solutions.

Open source is incredibly useful and widespread for information technology hence equally crucial for data analytics in the enterprise. It is a type licensing agreement which allows the developers and users to freely use the software, modify it, develop new ways to improve it and integrate to larger projects.

Some of the most popular Big Data and Analytics platforms with associated tools are Google BigQuery, Hortonworks Data Platform, HP Bigdata, IBM Big Data, Microsoft Azure, SAP Bigdata Analytics, Teradata Bigdata Analytics, Amazon Web Services.

Managing mobile devices can be daunting from many angles. The life cycle for mobile devices can be much shorter than traditional computing and telecommunication devices.

Nowadays, workers have multiple mobile phones. Having multiple mobile devices per person may equate to thousands of mobile devices to consider at the enterprise level.

The security implications of mobile devices are massive challenges. They create many security vulnerabilities for enterprises.

Mobile business intelligence, also known as Mobile BI is an essential requirement for enterprises to stay competitive, open new markets, and create new revenue streams.

The reality is that we cannot do business without the use of mobile devices any more. Mobility is an essential part of the enterprise. It touches every aspect of the enterprise. We cannot have a digital workplace without proper mobility architecture in place.

Talent is essential in enterprise modernisation and transformation initiatives. We need to understand the value and importance of talent for our programs. Without calibre talent, our digital programs cannot progress and transform productively.

Building high-performance teams are critical for the success of these programs. We need to create proactive and engaged local technical teams and community of practices as give back activities.

We need to focus on both qualitative and quantitative measures for team success. We can manage across complex matrix structures in our organisations.

As metric oriented digital professionals, we need to use KPIs (Key Performance Indicators). We can use a team dashboard to see the trends and qualify and quantify progress in visual formats for the team members and the business stakeholders.

Enterprise Architects have strategic, architectural thinking, and design thinking skills. Domain Architects can architect a component or integrated components in their business units. Infrastructure Architects are responsible for the underlying infrastructure such as network, servers, storage, platforms, physical facilities such as data centres and communications. Application Architects understand the functionality, operability, supportability, integration, and migration of applications. The most common specialty areas are Security Architect, Data Architect, Information Architect, Network Architect, Mobility Architect, Workplace Architect.

Technical specialists have distinct technology expertise covering a broad spectrum of technologies in all technical domains. These specialists are technically eminent professionals in their chosen field.

Business Analysts are critical resources to translate business requirements to technical requirements working with business stakeholders, architects, and technical specialists.

Mentoring and coaching is a cultural shift and the essential requirement of modernising environments. There must be a constant nurturing and knowledge transfer from top to bottom.

As digital leaders, we must be catalysts for ongoing change and serve as an Agile Champion. Due to changing technologies, process and tools, as digital leaders, we need to learn rapidly and efficiently.

I attempted to show significant aspects and valuable considerations for digital intelligence using a structured approach. I hope you found the framework easy to follow and the content concise, uncluttered, informative, and easy-to-read.

I overemphasised the architectural rigour on purpose. We cannot compromise the rigour aiming to the quality of products and services as a target outcome for modernisation and transformation goals in the enterprise. However, there must be a delicate balance among architectural rigour, business value, and speed to market.

Applying a pragmatic approach to multiple substantial transformation initiatives and complex modernisations programs has been beneficial for me. The key point is using an incrementally progressing iterative approach to every aspect of modernisation initiatives, including people, processes, tools, and technologies as a whole.

I have full confidence that this book provided valuable insights into the broad topic of digital intelligence.

Appendix: Other Books by this Author

Architecting Digital Transformation

12-step Architectural Leadership Method

Enterprises are facing enormous challenges to respond to the rapid changes and growing demands of digital consumers globally. There is constant search to find solutions to the growing problems. The most optimal solution to address this problem is to architect our enterprise digital transformation requirements aligning with digital trends and innovative frameworks as described in this book with an articulated 12-step method.

Architecting digital transformations address the root causes of fundamental issues that we experience in the digital world. The proliferation of digital media in the form of images, sound, and videos created a massive demand for our infrastructure to scale globally. Relentless sharing of these media types creates an unsustainable load over the networks, applications, and other expensive infrastructure components unless an effective capacity plan is in place.

Based on my architectural thought leadership on various enterprise architecture initiatives, digital transformation, and modernisation engagements, with my accumulated body of knowledge and skills from practical settings, I want to share these learnings in a concise book with a specific 12-step method hoping to add value by contributing to the broader digital community and the progressing digital transformation initiatives.

I made every effort to make this book concise, uncluttered, and easy-to-read by removing technical jargons to make it readable by a broader audience who want to architect their digital transformation programs to align with the growing demands of their digital consumers. In this book, I highlight the problems from an architectural point of view, following established and emerging methods, and recommend effective solutions to address them in a methodical way.

What distinguishes this book from other books on the market is that I provide a practical framework and a methodical approach to architect your organisation's digital infrastructure, applications, data, security, and other components based on experience, aiming not to sell or endorse any products or services to you.

A Practical Guide for IoT Solution Architects

Architecting secure, agile, economic, highly available, well-performing IoT ecosystems

The focus of this book is to provide IoT solution architects with practical guidance and a unique perspective. Solution architects working in IoT ecosystems have an unprecedented level of responsibility at work; therefore, dealing with IoT ecosystems can be daunting.

As an experienced practitioner of this topic, I understand the challenges faced by the IoT solution architects. In this book, I have reflected upon my insights based on my solution architecture experience spread across three decades. In addition, this book can also guide other architects and designers who want to learn the architectural aspects of IoT and understand the key challenges and practical resolutions in IoT solution architectures. Each chapter focuses on the key aspects that form the framing scope for this book; namely, security, availability, performance, agility, and cost-effectiveness.

In this book, I have also provided useful definitions, a brief practical background on IoT and a guiding chapter on solution architecture development. The content is mainly practical; hence, it can be applied or be a supplemental input to the architectural projects at hand.

Architecting Big Data Solutions Integrated with IoT & Cloud

Create strategic business insights with agility

IoT, Big Data, and Cloud Computing are three distinct technology domains with overlapping use cases. Each technology has its own merits; however, the combination of three creates a synergy and the golden opportunity for businesses to reap the exponential benefits. This combination can create technological magic for innovation when adequately architected, designed, implemented, and operated.

Integrating Big Data with IoT and Cloud architectures provide substantial business benefits. It is like a perfect match. IoT collects real-time data. Big Data optimises data management solutions. Cloud collects, hosts, computes, stores, and disseminates data rapidly.

Based on these compelling business propositions, the primary purpose of this book is to provide practical guidance on creating Big Data solutions integrated with IoT and Cloud architectures. To this end, the book offers an architectural overview, solution practice, governance, and underlying technical approach for creating integrated Big Data, Cloud, and IoT solutions.

The book offers an introduction to solution architecture, three distinct chapters comprising Big

Data, Cloud, and the IoT with the final chapter, including conclusive remarks to consider for Big Data solutions. These chapters include essential architectural points, solution practice, methodical rigour, techniques, technologies, and tools.

Creating Big Data solutions are complex and complicated from multiple angles. However, with the awareness and guidance provided in this book, the Big Data solutions architects can be empowered to provide useful and productive solutions with growing confidence.

A Technical Excellence Framework for Innovative Digital Transformation Leadership

Transform enterprise with technical excellence, innovation, simplicity, agility, fusion, and collaboration

The primary purpose of this book is to provide valuable insights for digital transformational leadership empowered by technical excellence by using a pragmatic five-pillar framework. This empowering framework aims to help the reader understand the common characteristics of technical and technology leaders in a structured way.

Even though there are different types of leaders in broad-spectrum engaging in digital transformations, in this book, we only concentrate on excellent technical and technology leaders having digital transformation goals to deal with technological disruptions and robust capabilities to create new revenue streams. No matter whether these leaders may hold formal executive titles or just domain specialist titles, they demonstrate vital characteristics of excellent technical leadership capabilities enabling them to lead complex and complicated digital transformation initiatives.

The primary reason we need to understand technical excellence and required capabilities for digital transformational leadership in a structured context is to model their attributes and transfer the well-known characteristics to the aspiring leaders and the next generations. We can transfer our understanding of these capabilities at an individual level and apply them to our day to day activities. We can even turn them into useful habits to excel in our professional goals. Alternatively, we can pass this information to other people that we are responsible for, such as our teenagers aiming for digital leadership roles, tertiary students, mentees, and colleagues.

We attempt to define the roles of strategic technical and technology leaders using a specific framework, based on innovation, simplicity, agility, collaboration, fusion and technical excellence. This framework offers a common understanding of the critical factors of the leader. The structured analysis presented in this book can be valuable to understand the contribution of technical leaders clearly.

Admittedly, this book has a bias towards the positive attributes of excellent leaders on purpose. The compelling reason for this bias is to focus on the positive aspects and describe these attributes concisely in an adequate amount to grasp the topic so that these positive attributes can be reused and modelled by the aspiring leaders. As the other side of the coin is also essential for different insights, I plan to deal with the detrimental aspects of useless leaders in a separate book, perhaps under the lessons learned context considering different use cases for a different audience type. Consequently, I excluded the negative aspects of useless leaders in this book.

A Modern Enterprise Architecture Approach

Transform enterprise with pragmatic architecture using mobility, IoT, Big Data, Cloud (Revised Edition)

I authored this book to provide essential guidance, compelling ideas, and unique ways to Enterprise Architects so that they can successfully perform complex enterprise modernisation initiatives transforming from chaos to coherence. This is not an ordinary theory book describing Enterprise Architecture in detail. There are myriad of books on the market and in libraries discussing details of

enterprise   architecture.
As a practising Senior Enterprise Architect, myself,
I read hundreds of those books and articles to learn
different views. They have been valuable to me to
establish my foundations in the earlier phase of my
profession. However, what is missing now is a
concise guidance book showing Enterprise
Architects the novel approaches, insights from the
real-life experience and experimentations, and
pointing out the differentiating technologies for
enterprise modernisation. If only there were such a
guide when I started engaging in modernisation
and   transformation   programs.
The biggest lesson learned is the business outcome
of the enterprise modernisation. What genuinely
matters for business is the return on investment of
the enterprise architecture and its monetising
capabilities. The rest is the theory because
nowadays sponsoring executives, due to economic
climate, have no interest, attention, or tolerance for
non-profitable ventures. I am sorry for
disappointing some idealistic Enterprise Architects,
but with due respect, it is the reality, and we cannot
change it. This book deals with reality rather than
theoretical perfection. Anyone against this view on
this climate must be coming from another planet.
In this concise, uncluttered and easy-to-read book, I
attempt to show the significant pain points and
valuable   considerations   for   enterprise
modernisation using a structured approach. The
architectural rigour is still essential. We cannot

compromise the rigour aiming to the quality of products and services as a target outcome. However, there must be a delicate balance among architectural rigour, business value, and speed to market. I applied this pragmatic approach to multiple substantial transformation initiatives and complex modernisations programs. The key point is using an incrementally progressing iterative approach to every aspect of modernisation initiatives, including people, processes, tools, and technologies as a whole. Starting with a high-level view of enterprise architecture to set the context, I provided a dozen of distinct chapters to point out and elaborate on the factors which can make a real difference in dealing with complexity and producing excellent modernisation initiatives. As eminent leaders, Enterprise Architects are the critical talents who can undertake this massive mission using their people and technology skills, in addition to many critical attributes such as calm and composed approach. They are architects, not firefighters. I have full confidence that this book can provide valuable insights and aha moments for these talented architects to tackle this enormous mission turning chaos to coherence.

About the Author

Dr Mehmet Yildiz is a Distinguished Enterprise Architect L3 certified from the Open Group. Working in the IT industry over the last 35 years, he recently focuses on cutting edge technology solutions, such as IoT, Blockchain, Cognitive, Cloud, Fog, and Edge Computing. He is a hands-on practitioner for solution architectures leading complex corporate projects and an Agile champion. As an innovation evangelist in all walks of life, he is also a recognised inventor. Mehmet teaches the best architectural practices at work, mentors his colleagues, supervises doctoral students, and provides industry-level lectures to postgraduate students at several universities in Australia. You can contact the author from his author platform https://digitalmehmet.com

www.ingramcontent.com/pod-product-compliance
Lightning Source LLC
Chambersburg PA
CBHW021405210526
45463CB00001B/222